PHOTOGRAPHY YEAR

1975 EDITION

BY THE EDITORS OF TIME-LIFE BOOKS

TIME-LIFE BOOKS, NEW YORK

ON THE COVER: A striking color study and a remarkable new lens tell the story of photography's artistic and technical accomplishments during 1974. The very long focal length lens—600mm—is one fifth the size of conventional telephoto lenses, its compact solid-glass structure made possible by computer techniques that are revolutionizing optical design. The picture of a woman with a cigarette, taken by Swiss-born photographer Hans Feurer, was part of an exhibit that drew special attention to color photography at Photokina in 1974.

Contents

It was the year for color in photography. During 1974, 389 dazzling color prints stole the art show at Photokina, the biennial fair held in Cologne, Germany, and color equipment filled Photokina's technological exhibits as well as supply shops around the world.

The increased emphasis on color was noticeable in the favor it found among photography's newly important patrons, the large international corporations. The work of some of the world's leading photographers found a major market in 1974 in enhancing the image of big business: documenting annual reports, filling pages of corporate publications, decorating the offices and lobbies of corporate headquarters. And much of this enhancement depended on color.

Color also seemed more important to promising young photographers. For the first time in PHOTOGRAPHY YEAR's annual showcase of new talent, two of the year's winners were chosen for their mastery of color.

The intensified interest in color owes much to new equipment that gives superb results with relatively simple procedures. In 1974, four manufacturers brought out comparatively inexpensive color enlargers of such simplicity and reliability that successful color printing became firmly established in the home.

But improved color enlarging was only part of the news in a year marked by numerous technological developments. Most significant was the impact on lens design of the computer, which has shortened the time needed to compute the form of a lens. A number of radical lens types came on the market in 1974. And multiple layers of microscopic coatings that virtually eliminate flare seemed to become the standard for high-quality lenses.

Countering this bright news, however, was one technological fact that became disturbingly clear in 1974: silver, the essential ingredient in all modern photographic processes, is a problem metal. It is swiftly rising in cost, and the chemicals needed to process silver-based materials harm the environment. It remains to be seen if the technology that can produce ever more automatic cameras and can revolutionize the home darkroom can find a way out of the silver crisis—and help photography survive.

The Editors

The Major Shows / 1

The Major Shows/1

Photokina/ BRANKO LENART, JR.: *Actor on the deck of the ferryboat Veneto*

A Feast of Color at Photokina

Color photography, almost ignored by museum directors for years, received a brilliant tribute at the biennial photo fair in Cologne

By far the largest and most important exhibition of color prints in 1974 was offered at Photokina, the international photography fair held every other year in Cologne, Germany. At the city's Gallery of Art, where the esthetic side of the fair was presented, color blazed from every corner. Near the entrance, a giant 47-by-11-foot color print covered one wall and part of the ceiling. Not far away, in a series of small, black-paneled chambers, color prints by eight outstanding professionals were displayed like gems in jewelry store windows. And a hallway running halfway around the gallery was lined with innovative color work by young photographers, mainly West Germans.

This magnificent display of color photography, unprecedented in Photokina's 25-year history, reflected the high regard in which color is held by the exhibition director, Professor L. Fritz Gruber. Photokina's commitment to color was a welcome rarity among last year's exhibitions of photography. Color photography has been bypassed by museums throughout the world. The expense of enlarging color transparencies to make high-quality prints prevents most curators from mounting large-scale shows in color. There is also an element of risk: a $200 print fades under the searing lights of an exhibition hall. Color photography's association with commercial work may also make it suspect to the purist photography establishment.

But it is certain that color photography now has a stronger grip on the imaginations of photographers and their viewers than at any other time since modern color-reversal film was introduced, almost 40 years ago. Provided with an ample budget, Gruber mounted a group of color exhibitions which were as up to date in their own way as the simultaneous trade show of the latest photographic equipment *(pages 108-114),* which occurred across town at Cologne's fair grounds.

Gruber presented over 350 color prints in five shows. Color's Challenge, a contest open to amateur and professional photographers 25 years old and under, included 180 prints chosen from 7,000 entries. In a second exhibition, Aspects of Photography, Gruber presented a series of ten dazzling one-man shows, all but one in color, to "demonstrate a widely individualistic range of image makers." Ten Commandments, an all-color exhibition that filled one large room, used contemporary photography to comment, sometimes ironically, on the relevance of biblical morality to today's world. Another contest, Focus on Play, featured photographs of children, some of them in color. Perhaps the most spectacular display of color presented 17 versions of the same mural-sized portrait, representing stages in the photographic developing process—from ghostly emergence out of a white background to final eclipse into blackness. "Color," said Gruber in the exhibition catalogue, "makes a decisive contribution to the physical things of our day, and with color film, we have been given a perfect material to record what we see."

A sleek Paris bus glides past an ornate
sculptured figure on one of the city's famous
bridges. This contrast of past and present
is one of 11 pictures exhibited by the Spanish-
born photographer at Photokina.

FRANCISCO HIDALGO: *Invalides Bridge in Paris*, 1967

The colorful turbulence of a medieval
tournament is re-created in modern Tokyo as the
white-helmeted members of a left-wing
movement, demanding the ouster of American
troops from Okinawa, battle against a black
phalanx of policemen. In their jousting with the
police, the protestors used huge, banner-
bearing bamboo spears as lances.

BRUNO BARBEY: *Tokyo riot*, 1971

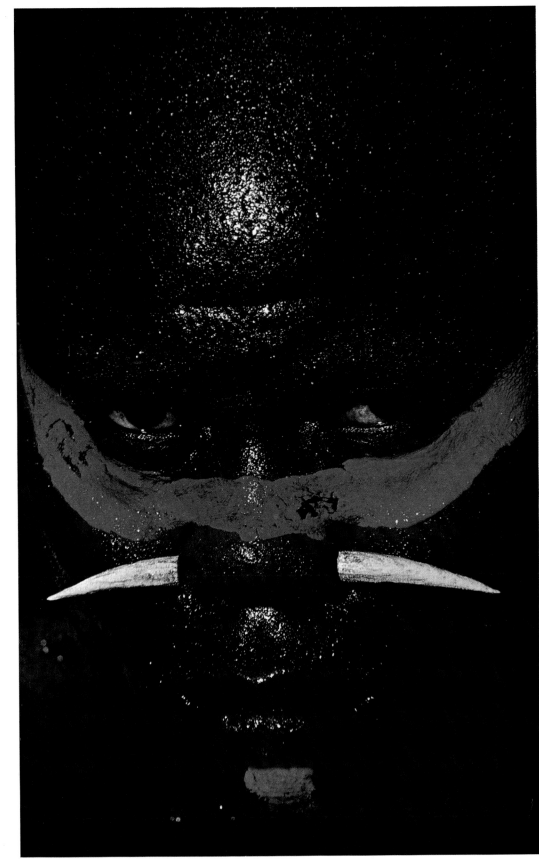

This streaked, scowling, bone-pierced face, resembling the fearsome visage of an African witch doctor, actually belongs to a black taxi driver in London. The picture is part of a series of advertising photographs on the theme of occultism, taken by one of Europe's most successful commercial photographers.

HANS FEURER: *Portrait for an advertisement*, 1970

HANS FEURER: *Portrait for a calendar*, 1973

Sulking under the shadow of her wide-brimmed hat, a woman becomes a study in browns and reds in a portrait made for an Italian calendar. A filter enabled the photographer to produce the highlights that shine like stars from the model's lips.

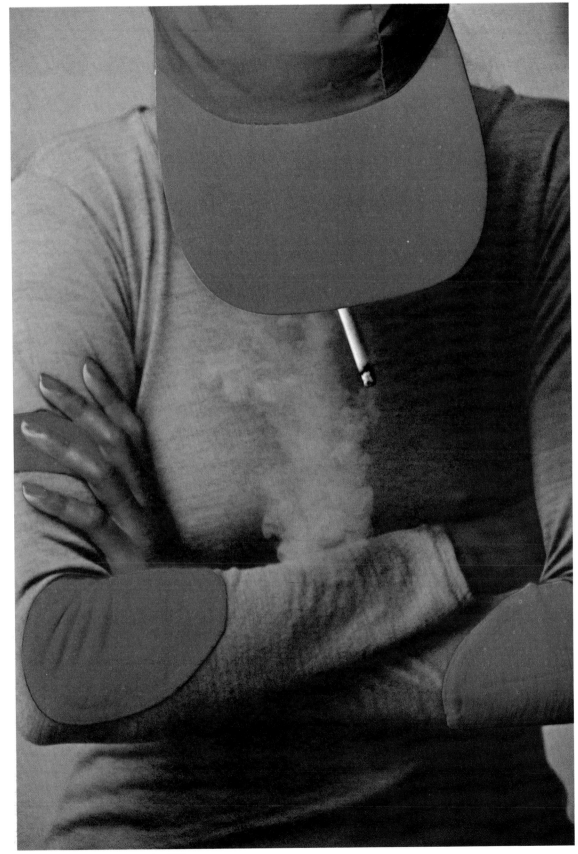

The model's costume, vibrant as a jockey's riding silks, is the true subject of this photograph taken for a German magazine. To catch the swirling cigarette smoke against the rich colors of the clothes, the photographer used an electronic flash.

HANS FEURER: *Magazine illustration,* 1970

Blackened to blend with the dark interior
of his armored car, a British soldier's face
betrays anxiety despite its stoic mask
of camouflage. The photograph was taken in the
Roman Catholic city of Newry, in Northern
Ireland, during an anti-British demonstration.

MICHAEL ABRAMSON: *British soldier in Northern Ireland,* 1972

The subtle distinctions in texture and tone between male and female flesh are captured in this picture of an embracing couple. The photographer posed his models outdoors, in the Italian countryside, so the natural light would enhance the warm skin colors.

SSILO TROST: *Couple*, 1972

*Areas of rich color add unexpected
relief to the otherwise bleak façade of an
abandoned building with its faded
political posters in Baltimore, Maryland.*

TOMAS SENNETT: *For Rent*, 1973

The elements of a typical urban scene—a bike rider, a stop sign, and a fireplug in Troy, New York—suddenly become an arrangement of form and color as perfectly composed and precisely rendered as a painting. In fact, the photographer says he never poses or adjusts his subjects; instead, he travels the United States on the alert for just such happenstance patterns.

TOMAS SENNETT: *Stop Sign*, 1972

A New Breed of Photographers at San Francisco

Not one style but many marked a huge show that documented the free-swinging approach developing on the U.S. West Coast

Forty-two years ago, an exhibition at San Francisco's M. H. de Young Memorial Museum introduced a new style of photography. Among the exhibitors were some of the great names of American photography—Edward Weston, Imogen Cunningham, and Ansel Adams, all living in northern California. These photographers were members of the f/64 Group—named for the smallest available aperture on view cameras, a setting that provides extremely fine focus and maximum depth of field. The group's name thus symbolized the sharply realized, unmanipulated style of nature and nude photography that has dominated West Coast photography since the '30s.

In recent years, however, a different look in California photography has been developing, and in the spring of 1974 it surfaced in New Photography: San Francisco and the Bay Area—a big, provocative show at the de Young Memorial, the same museum that housed the first exhibition of the older tradition. In a broad sense, the 1974 show summarized changes of attitudes that have been imported from all over the U.S. and have developed in California: a departure from the keen-honed discipline of the f/64 Group; an introspection that may be a reaction from the social activism of the 1960s; and an eclecticism partly based on the restlessness of young Americans. More than 400 works by 23 photographers were shown. Though all the photographers—most of them under 35—lived in the San Francisco Bay area, some had moved there from as far away as Massachusetts and Georgia.

A newcomer to the Bay area, the show's organizer, Thomas H. Garver, Curator of Exhibitions at the Fine Arts Museums of San Francisco, assumed that he would find a single new "high style" of San Francisco photography as trend-setting as the old f/64 tradition. He looked at the portfolios of about 120 photographers before narrowing the field down to the 23 actually shown. Then he stepped aside and let each photographer decide for himself what he would show and how.

The result took Garver by surprise. Though it did represent a clear break with the older California tradition, it did not add up to a single new style. On the contrary, New Photography was a grab bag of recent trends, from the experimental to the traditional. At one end of the show's wide range were mixed-media works employing such nonphotographic materials as slices of bread and fabric. At the other end were straight photographic prints of lyrical beauty. Between the extremes, the coolly documentary coexisted with the intensely subjective.

One of the best known of the photographers shown was Kenneth Graves, a freelance photojournalist whose work has appeared in *Camera, Ramparts* and *Rolling Stone*. Graves, 32, is one of a new breed of young photographers who have set themselves the task of documenting ordinary life in America in a detached, almost clinical spirit. In New Photography he exhibited a group of black-and-white prints from a series of pictures he has made of high school football teams. Unlike the usual sports photographer, Graves did not concentrate on the action and excitement of the game itself. Instead, he showed the intervals between plays, and the quiet moments before and after the game: during the huddle, on the sidelines, in the locker room. The result did not display the usual preoccupation with athletic prowess, but a penetrating and skeptical study of the fatigue, uncertainty and fear that each individual player must overcome if the team is to win.

Georgia-born Crawford Barton, 31, is also interested in photographing real life, but his approach to it is lyrical and subjective. He concentrates on the homosexual community of San Francisco, an area of life that is strange and disturbing to most people. In some of his pictures that strangeness comes through. In others, however, Barton celebrates the simple joys and sorrows that all human beings share with one another.

One of a growing number of younger photographers who have turned their backs on reportage and documentation, 28-year-old Ellen Brooks has adapted old photographic techniques to the creation of works that are strikingly contemporary. "Bread Spreads," the work Ellen Brooks contributed to New Photography, consists of three large panels suggesting quilted bedcovers, and made of photosensitized fabric. Each of the first two panels is composed of 380 small squares of cloth, printed directly from slices of bread, and then stitched together. The slices of bread are whole in the first panel, but in the second they are broken into small pieces. The third panel was printed on a single muslin sheet on which the photographer dropped crumbs of the bread used in the first two. To produce "Bread Spreads," Brooks made use of a photographic process that dates from the earliest days of photography: the photogram. A photogram is produced by placing an object on the surface of a material that has been chemically treated to make it photosensitive, and exposing object and material to light. The object, by blocking light from the material, acts like a negative; when the object is removed, its imprint remains.

Almost as nonpersonal as "Bread Spreads"—though technically more orthodox—are the calm, empty landscapes of Gary Stewart, 38. Stewart, a Minnesota-born bartender who has lived in San Francisco for the past six years, points his camera at the real world and prints the results in the ordinary way on photographic paper. However, people seldom appear in his pictures, and sometimes his camera records empty space with landscape or architecture merely providing a frame. In all his pictures, abstract elements of light and composition are more important than subject matter; most of his photographs create a mood of mysterious expectation.

Twenty-five-year-old Leslie Poliak photographs unsmiling girls and young men dressed up in costumes or playing parts in imaginary dramas. Her

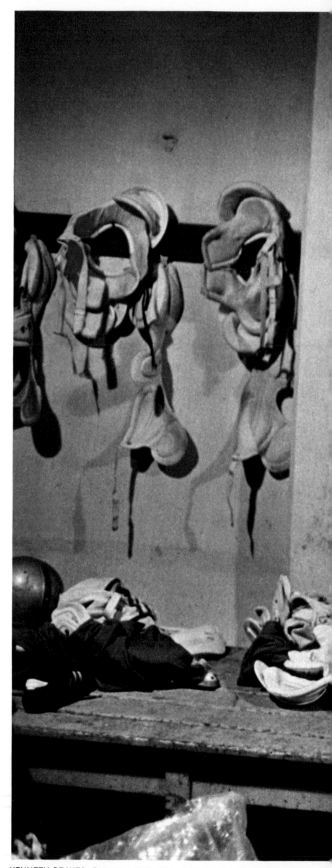

strangely disturbing pictures suggest—without explicitly stating—bizarre erotic fantasies. People are central to her photographs but her approach to them does not reflect the reportorial viewpoint of a documentary photographer. Instead, Poliak plans her pictures in advance, drawing on her dreams and daydreams for subject matter. Then, when she finds the right models, she costumes and poses them. She thinks of each photograph as a little movie and directs her models, whom she treats like actors, as a film director would. The results are often as suggestive and enigmatic as a still from a foreign movie whose plot is unknown.

Though William Messer, 26, uses his camera as a kind of diary to document the important moments of his life, he departs from realism by focusing on some external symbol that summarizes the moment instead of trying to explain it—expressing his almost mystical sense of the role of photography in life. To the casual observer his pictures of empty rooms, friends and urban landscapes might look as trivial as snapshots or the kind of picture that gets taken when film is exposed accidentally at the beginning or end of a roll. A closer look may tease the viewer with hints and suggestions of meaning that are seldom clearly conveyed. To Messer, however, the pictures have a unique significance that relates them to the deepest mysteries of human existence.

In a show as large and varied as New Photography, trend spotters might have difficulty—as Curator Garver did—discovering an overall pattern. However, Garver points out one significant characteristic of the younger photographers: their quiescent self-absorption. "They are not interested in making a socially significant document in the grand tradition of Cartier-Bresson and W. Eugene Smith. They're more interested in the events and circumstances of their own lives." This inward-looking quiescence is most evident in photographers with a strongly personal and subjective approach, but even the most straightforwardly documentary of the new San Francisco Bay area photographers are careful not to lose their cool.

On a gymnasium bench littered with helmets, jerseys and protective padding, a high school football player braces his legs and cocks his arm like a Roman gladiator at his moment of triumph in the Colosseum. Though such locker room clowning is a commonplace of team sports, Graves's cool camera suggests that the victim may be the youthful gladiator himself.

KENNETH GRAVES: *Defensive Back, George Washington High Eagles, 1970*

Two girls joyfully deck each other with flowers in a pool of clear water. This idyllic picture was made in the Mojave Desert, where a cool stream tempts campers to bathe nude.

CRAWFORD BARTON: *Deep Creek*, 1970

triking a note of ambiguity in a classic
atement on the theme of freedom in nature,
 long line of jagged fence seems to confine a
oung man running naked in a field. The
icture was made near the California coast.

CRAWFORD BARTON: *Untitled*, 1972

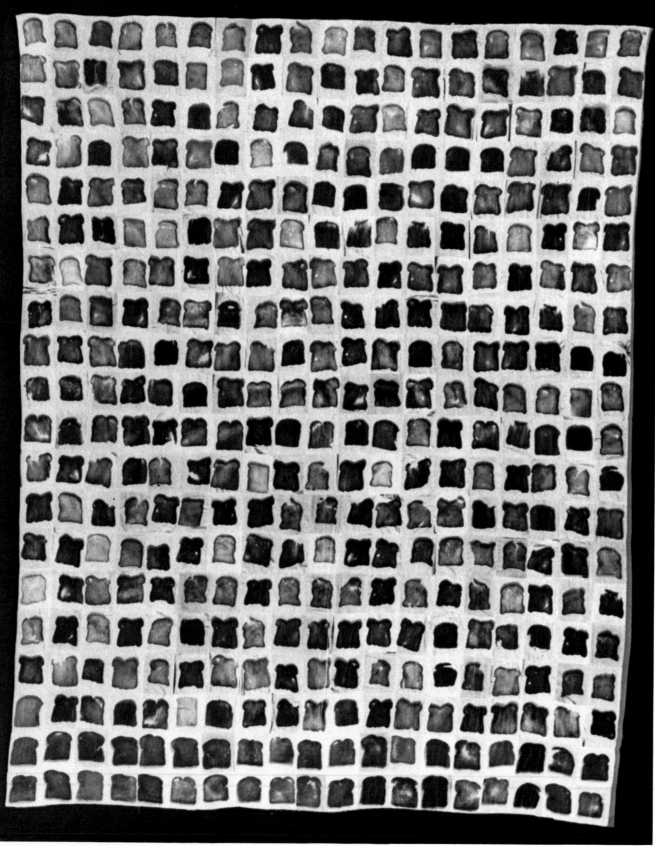

ELLEN BROOKS: *Bread Spread I*, 1974

Measuring 8 feet by 10 feet, this large wall hanging is the first of a series of three in which the photographer combined pieces of bread with photosensitized cloth and printed directly on the material. To achieve the "toasty" tones of the bread in the resulting print, she cut some slices thinner than others, letting different amounts of light through. The whole project used 10 loaves of bread.

Precisely composed by the photographer
on a rainy-day walk in New York, an arrangement
of white-topped restaurant tables on the
textured carpet of a deserted hotel patio is
basically an abstraction. Yet the picture also
suggests the mysterious enchantment of a
toy shop after hours; as in a fairy tale, the tables
might almost be spinning tops, or hoop-skirted
doll dancers poised for a minuet.

GARY STEWART: *Untitled,* 1972

A girl—whose face suggests a young boy pretending to be a girl—strikes an awkward attitude in a feather boa and glittery gold dress. The photographer, interested in what she calls "the fine line between masculine and feminine," chose the 15-year-old model precisely because of her boyish good looks. The posture and costume enhance an atmosphere of sexual fantasy.

LESLIE POLIAK: *Untitled*, 1973

A pretty girl whose curly hair hugs her head like a helmet frowns slightly and cups her hands over the eyes of a German shepherd dog. Perhaps the girl is merely caressing the dog. But maybe she sees something disturbing and wishes to shield him from the sight. Like a still from a phantom movie that no one will ever see, the picture suggests a story line that will never be told.

LESLIE POLIAK: *Untitled*, 1973

WILLIAM MESSER: *Peter under the Lamppost*, 1973

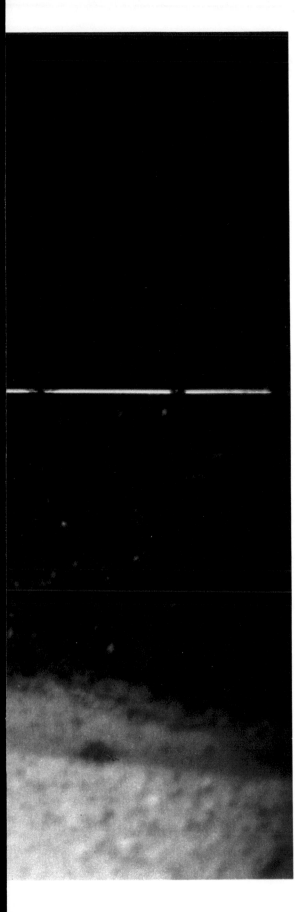

On a dark, silent street a young man leans
against a lamppost and gazes at a house across
the way. In the 15 seconds that it took to make
this photograph, a passing car left a streak
of light like a river of quicksilver on the street.
The picture captures the poignant, brooding
tension of an endless evening in which nothing
happens but everything seems possible.

Tribute from Minor White

In "Celebrations," last of a series of exhibitions, a famous and controversial photographer-teacher provided a showcase for depicters of the joy and solemnity of life

One way to start a fight among photographers is to mention the name of Minor White, director—with Jonathan Green—of the exhibition "Celebrations" at the Massachusetts Institute of Technology. Celebrations was the last of a series of exhibitions that Minor White organized for the Hayden Gallery of M.I.T. He retired as Professor of Photography in 1974 to write and photograph, though he will return as professor emeritus after a year. Like all Minor White exhibitions, Celebrations was deeply imbued with the personality and philosophy of a man about whom a moderate opinion seems impossible. His admirers approach him with an attitude that verges at times on religious adoration. Others, baffled by his austere photographs, his poeticizing, and his Pied Piper of Hamelin effect on old and young alike sometimes turn on him in frustrated fury.

No one denies, however, that Minor White is a force to be reckoned with in American photography today. For 22 years as editor of Aperture, a small-circulation quarterly magazine of high artistic standards, he has launched many young photographers and influenced the publication of some of the finest photography books in recent years. As a teacher at M.I.T., the Rochester Institute of Technology and numerous workshops, and as organizer of exhibitions at M.I.T. and George Eastman House, he has brought a new understanding of photography to thousands of amateurs and professionals alike. Through his teaching he has been able to educate those who look at photographs along with those who take them, and then bring the two groups together in a series of beautifully produced exhibitions and publications—in itself enough to guarantee his following.

However, Minor White's influence rests not so much on the teaching positions he has occupied as on the moral force he has exerted through them. To hundreds if not thousands of photographers, photography students and photography lovers, Minor White is a saintly prophet and seer of a faith without which their lives would be cold, empty, and gray.

Minor White reached this eminence by a long and circuitous route that began in Minneapolis. Born in 1908, White became interested in photography at the age of eight, though his studies at the University of Minnesota were concentrated in writing and botany. When he took up photography seriously, in the late 1930s, he worked as a documentary photographer for a government agency and as a publicity photographer for a civic theater. It was not until he was nearly 40 that Minor White really set foot on his present path.

This step was taken through the influence of Alfred Stieglitz, who was 82 years old and in the last year of his life when Minor White first met him. Stieglitz had long since ceased publication of his magazine Camera Work; sick and alone, he was living near his last gallery, An American Place. However, his message had already spread through a small group of serious photog-

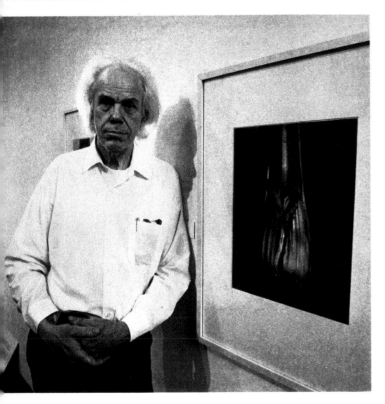

*inor White, who retired from his post as
rofessor of Photography at the Massachusetts
Institute of Technology in 1974, stands beside
n exhibit in M.I.T.'s Hayden Gallery during the
photographic show "Celebrations." On the
all beside him is a work by Joe DeMaio, one of
e 65 contributors to the exhibition.*

raphers that included Minor White. For White, the seminal Stieglitz concept was the idea that a photograph of a cloud, an eroded rock or a bit of frozen fern could be a symbol or metaphor for the photographer's deepest perceptions of goodness and truth. Minor White's gradual understanding of this idea was the beginning of his present work in photography. In 1946, the year he met Stieglitz, he began a heavy schedule of teaching, photographing, exhibitions, and participation in seminars that led to the foundation of *Aperture* in 1952 and to his eventual appointment in 1965 as Visiting Professor of Photography at M.I.T. That such a mystic as Minor White could teach at a school some have called a "university polarized around science" is paradoxical, but M.I.T. takes the incongruity in stride. "We've been working a long time toward a more inclusive vision of what is important in the life of a student, and we have made a determined effort to include a number of arts programs," explains Professor Donlyn Lyndon, head of the Architecture Department in which Minor White taught. For M.I.T., as for Minor White, the role of a photography teacher is not to train professional photographers but to develop creative vision and expression.

The exhibitions Minor White organized at M.I.T. have played an important part in his teaching activity. In Celebrations, photographers as famous as Imogen Cunningham and Minor White himself were shown side by side with young unknowns in groupings expressive of White's own personal philosophy. The idea was to express the joy and solemnity of life in photographs. Few of the pictures chosen depicted actual celebrations such as New Year's Eve or Easter. Most of them were, to use the Stieglitz word favored by White, equivalents, or metaphors, for the quiet or jubilant feelings aroused by aspects of nature or human life.

The exhibition runs the gamut from near abstraction to crisp reportage, and contains works of photographers young and old, established and obscure. The youngest photographer shown in the selection on the following pages is 25-year-old Carl Leavitt, who lives in rural Maine with his wife and has only been photographing for four years. The oldest photographer is Imogen Cunningham, at 91 the dean of living American photographers, who took her first picture in 1901. One of the founding members of the f/64 Group, she had her 34th one-man show in 1974 at the Santa Barbara Museum of Art in California.

The other photographers shown here—Michael Kaufman, 41, Terry Reed, 26, John Loori, 43, and Siegfried Halus, 31—all share Minor White's view of photography as a way of making contact with the deeper aspects of life. Discussing his picture of a jazz musician and his wife embracing *(pages 38-39)*, Michael Kaufman says, "It's an image of the spirit, a moment of recognition that all life is a continuing celebration of life itself."

CARL LEAVITT: *Untitled,* 1973

In this famous close-up of a flower, the graceful curves of the magnolia's petals, backlit and glowing, set off the cone of the stamen and pistil. Best known of Cunningham's photographs of plant forms from the 1920s, this study in design is also a celebration of the forces of life.

In a picture imbued with the delicacy of a Chinese painting, a maple branch is silhouetted against mossy streams of limestone, which has dissolved and flowed out of cracks in an old concrete bridge abutment. The photographer waded up to his waist in water to get the right vantage point.

MOGEN CUNNINGHAM: *Magnolia blossom*, 1925

The tenderness and trust of married love is captured in this informal photograph. The man, a saxophone player in a band at a Berkeley, California hotel, kisses his wife gently on the cheek during a break in the music.

MICHAEL KAUFMAN: *Eddie and His Wife*, 1973

Two Muscovy ducks waddle across a lawn in the shade of a butternut tree. In this bucolic view of a farm in Illinois, the atmosphere of rural peace is enhanced by the use of infrared film, which lightens the sunlit leaves and increases the contrast between them and the shaded lawn.

TERRY REED: *Untitled,* 1972

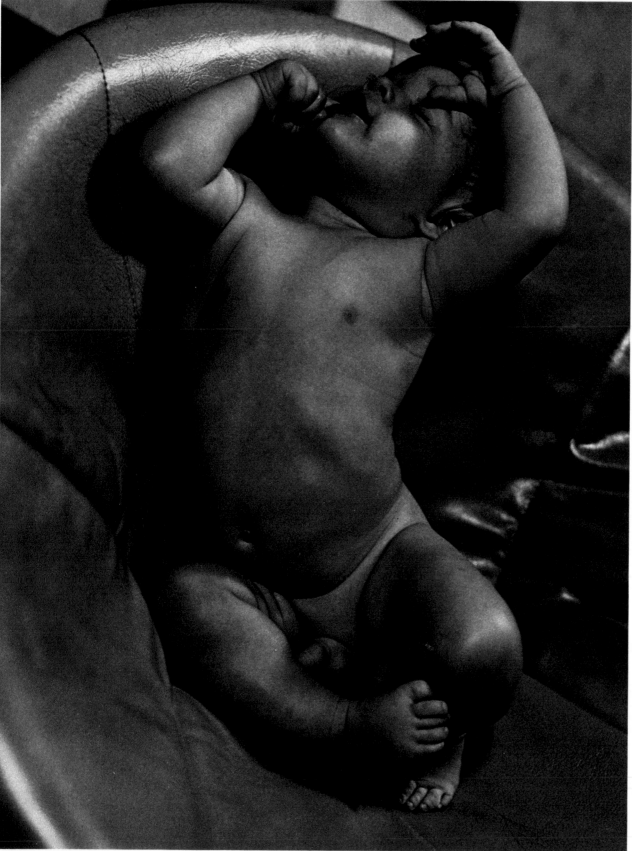

JOHN LOORI: *Asian's Moment*, 1973

A baby squirms ecstatically in celebration of the joys of infancy. The photographer placed his seven-month-old son in a vinyl-covered chair and played with him for an hour to get this shot.

The three faces in this picture taken at New York's
Metropolitan Museum of Art all look carved—
though one belongs to a bearded old man and
the others are of limestone from ancient Cyprus.

SIEGFRIED HALUS: *Untitled*, 1970

Plastic roses left on the lid of a marble coffin represent the paradoxes of mortality. The stone is worn and weathered by time, while the man-made flowers preserve their lushness intact. The metal rings on the lid allow the coffin to be opened and other bodies added. The picture was taken in a Catholic cemetery in Puerto Rico.

MINOR WHITE: *Rings and Roses*, 197

Laughlin's Enigmatic Lost World

In a moody and lyrical one-man show, a photographer of architecture proved he had always been after something far more significant

The fantastic poetic visions of Clarence John Laughlin have never been better seen than in the 229-picture retrospective that closed early in 1974 at the Philadelphia Museum of Art. The exhibit spanned the entire range of Laughlin's career since the mid-1930s. Ante-bellum mansions crumbling into ruins, windup phonographs, wall clocks and stuffed birds, children and mysterious women from the half-forgotten byways of the Old South: these are a few of the elements out of which Laughlin has built an intensely personal world that is both strange and familiar.

Best known as an architectural photographer, Laughlin has traveled all over the United States on a one-man crusade to record vanishing Victorian buildings for posterity, and his book on old Louisiana plantations, *Ghosts Along the Mississippi,* is still in print more than 25 years after its original publication. From the beginning of his career, Laughlin has preferred tripod-mounted view cameras, valuable for the sharp pictures they produce. However, even his most literal records of old buildings have an air of mystery and magic that transcends the documentary, while many of his most characteristic pictures are not architectural documents at all, but elegiac still lifes and figure studies that evoke times past and lost worlds. In the Aperture monograph that served as the catalogue for the show, Laughlin writes: "The mystery of time, the magic of light, the enigma of reality—and their interrelationships—are my constant themes and preoccupations."

Born in 1905 in Lake Charles, Louisiana, Clarence John Laughlin now lives in New Orleans. He started out as a part-time writer and bank clerk before he began photographing still lifes in 1935. During the next few years, Laughlin photographed the statues, cemeteries and old buildings of New Orleans, and his first book, *New Orleans and Its Living Past,* was published in 1941. Since then he has had more than 200 one-man shows in museums and university art galleries throughout the country and has had his pictures published in *Vogue,* LIFE, *Mademoiselle, Architectural Review, American Heritage, Popular Photography, Aperture* and other periodicals.

This is hardly the career of an obscure photographer, and yet there is a sense in which Laughlin is unknown. His most popular pictures—of old plantations along the Mississippi—have so far outshadowed others in the public mind that, to many, the Philadelphia show came as a revelation of both the diversity and the underlying unity of his work. Laughlin himself emphasizes his highly personal, extremely romantic approach. He believes that the world is far stranger than most people think, and that what some regard as reality is only a small part of a larger "total reality." To Laughlin, the physical object is "merely a steppingstone to an inner world. . . . By dealing with the object in this way, the creative photographer sets free the *human contents* of objects and imparts humanity to the inhuman world around him."

With a resigned air, a veiled woman reclines on a bed whose mattress resembles an animal's snout. The cracked wall, broken windowpanes, and rubble symbolize a marriage without love.

The Repulsive Bed, 1941

The Enigma, 1941

Bushes and vines envelop the plastered brick columns and cast-iron Corinthian capitals of this Mississippi plantation house, mysteriously destroyed by fire in the 1890s. Clouds over the ruins form a question mark.

Birds built a nest where the pendulum of this old clock used to swing, and after they left, spiders covered the nest with cobwebs. Laughlin found the clock in a partly abandoned house in Louisiana.

And Tell of Time . . . Cobwebbed Time, 1947

Plantation Boy, 1951

The hoe, hats and palmetto fan in this carefully composed picture suggest the mixed origins of this young plantation worker, a descendant of blacks and the French who pioneered in Louisiana.

A dignified woman, the leader of a
religious cult tinged with voodooism,
stands before one of the massive,
vaulted walls of her sect's meeting place
in an old New Orleans neighborhood.

"Mother" Brown, 1945

51

Milwaukee Nostalgic Still Life, 1964

A turn-of-the-century phonograph with a "morning glory" horn, and a glass drugstore jar on a gilded cast-iron stand are arranged to evoke an age that reveled in ornate decoration.

A cardboard Victorian doll and plastic
babies taped to a piece of driftwood
create a satire on overpopulation
—its title inspired by James Joyce.

Haveth Childers Everywhere, 1952

53

This stuffed bird, surrounded by flowers made of ribbons, was placed in a wooden box with a glass front by an anonymous craftsman and left at a gravesite as a memorial for the dead.

Bird of the Death Dream, 1953

The Marketplace / 2

The Marketplace/2

The Corporate Image/ JAY MAISEL: *PepsiCo World Headquarters, Purchase, New York*

The Marketplace

Polishing the Corporate Image

A special kind of patron, the multimillion-dollar corporation, is now challenging some of the country's top photographers with unusual pressures, problems—and pay

One of the last frontiers for romantic and adventurous photographic assignments is provided by—of all things—the multi-million-dollar corporations. Many of the giant companies that drill for oil under the high seas or the arctic tundra, haul wood out of mist-shrouded forests, send signals to space or open new markets in the U.S.S.R. have turned to top-notch photographers to make pictures at the scenes of their activities. Partly as a result of such assignments, and partly by haphazard circumstance, corporations have become major depositories of fine and unusual collections of photographs. And they have both the facilities and the finances to display their acquisitions in museum-quality exhibits. Last year some of them chose to do just that.

■ Exxon commissioned tens of thousands of dollars worth of photographic work for company reports and publications—and also maintained five traveling exhibits of art and photography that were sent on tour and have been displayed in some 40 cities in the United States.

■ In Redondo Beach, California, TRW Inc., an aerospace, electronics and automotive firm, maintains a photography department that produced exhibits of photographs for display in the public spaces of the company's own facilities; it did some $1 million worth of photographic business last year for TRW divisions as well as other corporations.

■ The nation's sixth largest utility, Commonwealth Edison, commissioned photographer Steffens Leinwohl to document a wide variety of urban and industrial themes. Leinwohl shot over a thousand pictures; 50 of them now hang on the walls of the utility's Chicago headquarters.

■ The nation's largest bank, Bank of America, assigned photographer Bob Foothorap to record the four-month labor of artists Jesus Campusano and Luis J. Cortazar as they painted a mural for a newly renovated branch of the bank in the Mission District of San Francisco. The mural was revealed in June—and so were Foothorap's striking black-and-white photographs of the artists' progress.

Many of the finest of the photographs owned and exhibited by corporations were taken on assignments made in somewhat narrower self-interest. The good corporation photographer finds himself in something like the situation of the medieval craftsman who adjusted his creative urge to the demands of a wealthy patron and worked a portrait of his patron into a stained-glass window or a stone carving. In present-day terms, the photographer must often steer a delicate course between photojournalism and the staged artifice of advertising. But the best of these photographers steer the course skillfully, and arrive at exciting solutions to this touchy problem.

Co Rentmeester found himself on the Danish island of Samsoe one cold and blustery autumn morning, attempting to show how a pharmaceutical product produced by Pfizer kept the island's pig population of 35,000 worm-free and healthy. Rentmeester soon realized that fashioning a silk purse out of the island slaughterhouse was not going to be easy: "A carcass is a carcass," he remembers thinking to himself as he searched for the right picture. He angled his shots to isolate slaughterhouse details and took each picture three times, using different filters to adjust for the harsh fluorescent lighting. Late in the afternoon, as he strolled about the island while waiting for the plane that took him back to Copenhagen, Rentmeester snapped a gentle portrait of a bearded veterinarian cuddling a pig in his arms. That picture, along with an abstract study in color *(page 66),* made the positive point that the Pfizer company wanted in its annual report: technology moves agriculture "closer to science."

Harald Sund is a young Seattle-based photographer who loves to backpack through the Northwest wilderness making lyrical pictures of alder-rimmed lakes and snow-tipped firs. Recently, on assignments from Louisiana-Pacific, the second-largest lumber producer in the U.S., Sund has traveled east of his home grounds, discovering a whole new set of skills and considerably widening the scope of his work. "I want emotional impact in my photographs," says Sund. "The company set up guidelines, then gave me a free hand." His evocative photography has illuminated the Louisiana-Pacific 1973 annual report, its first as a separate company since it was spun off from Georgia-Pacific. Again and again the report makes the point that the new company will not diversify from its main line of business—that it will "stay close to the tree." Sund's images of nature immensely strengthen that corporate rhetoric.

Many photographers find a whole new world opening up to them inside the corporate setting. Jay Maisel, a New York photographer who originally made his reputation with outdoor photography, now says enthusiastically: "I find factories, American industry in general, very exciting. Have you ever seen a quarter mile of steel ribbon running through a mill at 40 miles an hour? One time we walked into a mill and my young assistant took a look around, went up to a foreman and said, 'Man, if you put a glass roof over this place you'd have a discotheque that would make millions.' "

Corporations will pay such experienced and creative photographers as Maisel from $300 to $1,500 a day plus expenses. But in most cases the day-rate purchases ownership of all the pictures made during an assignment. While the photographer can often obtain permission to use his pictures for some other purpose, the companies are extremely cautious about what that other purpose might be. And though corporate photography is well paid, the scale is not as high as that of advertising work. Phil Marco, for example, can create an illusion as great as all outdoors in his small Manhattan studio, and

Photographic art (above) is part of the decorative scheme in most of the executive offices at the Squibb headquarters. This set of four subdued flower close-ups by St. Louis graphics designer and photographer Charles Reay, organized in a five-by-five-foot arrangement of dye-transfer prints, hangs in the controller's office.

Photography has begun to replace conventional graphics in corporate offices. In a ninth-floor reception area of the sleek new Manhattan offices of Joseph E. Seagram & Sons, the walls are adorned with a group of Aaron Siskind photographs on the theme of life in the city.

Last year E. R. Squibb & Sons presented "Eye of the Beholder," an exhibit of great color photographs, at its new world headquarters in Princeton, New Jersey. A local foundation that supports research on retina diseases benefited from contributions made at a private preview, and the exhibit later toured the U.S.

he gets as much as $3,000 a page for photographing products there to the tight specifications of an advertising layout. He gets half that amount, or less, for a page in an annual report. Nevertheless, he welcomes the other compensations: "I'm given a great deal of leeway—a full page to come up with my own concept. And I can work until I'm happy with what I have, re-take a picture over and over to get it right."

There are sometimes other dividends to the work as well, such as opportunities to meet and photograph the mighty. Last year Donald Kendall, Chairman of PepsiCo, took photographer Burt Glinn along to the U.S.S.R. for a trip that celebrated the company's coup in opening the Russian market to American soft drinks. Kendall was scheduled for a conference with Party Chairman Leonid Brezhnev, and Glinn shot pictures for 15 minutes as the two chairmen chatted and Brezhnev jovially—and unsuccessfully—tried to open a bottle of Pepsi-Cola in the old Russian way of opening a bottle of vodka, by slapping it sharply on the bottom. "He had to be a little curious about this photographer who kept reaching over his shoulder and turning the bottle so that the label would show," says Glinn.

Aside from such semi-documentary contributions to corporate literature, there is the role of photography in shaping a corporation's image of itself on its own premises. In the past, designers convinced entrepreneurs that good architecture and collections of fine art represented not only sound investments of capital but an equally sound investment in corporate image. Now designers are beginning to convince many executives that good photographic art—even when it has nothing to do with the company's line of business —sets a style of modernity in the corporate office.

The new world-wide headquarters of E. R. Squibb & Sons in Princeton, New Jersey, display some 300 large dye-transfer prints made chiefly from photographs by Ernst Haas that appeared in his 1971 book, *The Creation.* In Chicago's Exchange National Bank, a collection of prints, including originals by Steichen and Stieglitz, adorns the bank's public spaces and executive offices. The partners of the big Los Angeles law firm O'Melveny and Myers focused their collection on historic pictures of southern California and on scenes of western grandeur done by Ansel Adams and Edward Weston. In Manhattan, Joseph E. Seagram & Sons built its impressive new collection around an urban theme, including a Lewis Hine photograph of the Empire State Building and one by Berenice Abbott of the Flatiron Building.

The demand for such work will of course vary with the economy, since a corporation might cut back on this sort of expenditure first when times are bad. But over the long run, more and more corporation heads seem to be coming to the conclusion that their images are improved by collections of photographs—and that means more assignments for the best photographers.

Enhancing a Medium and its Message

The commonest and most striking contribution of photography to the corporate image in the past year has been the enhancement of that corporate symbol, the annual report —the company's message to its owners, the stockholders.

Often the glossy annual report results from the combined efforts of advertising experts and designers employed or assigned by the corporation. And the designers have tended to choose photographers whose work they have admired in the illustrated magazines. Working together in much the same way that a magazine editor and a photographer work to produce an attractive or compelling picture story, these designers and photographers have added an exciting new dimension to the annual report. By focusing intensely and with the eyes of an innocent on a company's products, the photographer has transformed workaday objects into heightened images. The annual report of carpet yarn-processors HCA-Martin, for instance, dwells on the company's exploration of ways to impart anti-static and flame-retardant properties to yarns. But the photograph by Gary Gladstone of a scramble of yarns *(page 69)* is pure romance.

If a photographer cannot simply find a corporate image, as Gladstone found one in a factory yarn bin, he creates it. Wallace-Murray is a $330-million amalgamation of businesses, some dating back to the early 19th Century, when they made tools for Yankee farmers. Photographer Ron Barnett went from one Wallace-Murray plant to another, assembling saws, gears, drills, faucets, ventilating pipes, and other products. His dazzling inventory of things mundane and useful, spread over 22 pages of the annual report, is proof that such objects can form gleaming abstract designs in spite of their precise detail.

Commissioned photography has also served to project a company's concern about its products, its employees, and its effect on the environment. When PepsiCo decided to move out of midtown Manhattan 10 years ago, the company chose architect Edward Durell Stone to design its new suburban offices and the surrounding landscape. Then, when the offices were opened, PepsiCo commissioned photographer Jay Maisel to evoke the quality of life at the new headquarters in a 28-page full-color booklet. Maisel's photographs, like the one of Canada geese floating on a lake *(page 57),* concentrate on the unspoiled environment and the sheer beauty of the new quarters.

One result of the new approach to corporate image making has been a truer, more straightforward approach—even in the case of a professional model. Thus a corporate image can be as direct, and as attractive, as the classically beautiful face in Revlon's annual report *(right),* looking the reader in the eye with unflinching honesty.

When the photographer asked model
Lauren Hutton for a "real" face, he got a direct,
no-nonsense look. This photograph of the
woman who is a $200,000-a-year trademark for a
line of cosmetics might have been a bit too
direct for an ad, but it was just right for the
company's 1973 annual report.

RICHARD AVEDON: *Revlon annual report*, 1973

Every winter hundreds of youngsters take to the slopes in PepsiCo-sponsored ski meets. This startling shot of spider-web cables, with young skiers in chair lifts ascending the flank of a mountain like a swarm of silhouetted insects, makes a point about the company's ski program in a fresh, unhackneyed way.

BURT GLINN: *PepsiCo ski meet,* 1973

A Paul Bunyan-sized pile of logs in an Idaho forest displays for Louisiana-Pacific's stockholders some of their company's $565 million worth of assets.

HARALD SUND: *Louisiana-Pacific timber*, 1973

*The problem: find a way to photograph
a pharmaceutical company's success with new
medicines to control animal parasites.
Pictures of hogs and worms would hardly do.
The photographer found his solution in
a glowing, gas-fired branding iron proudly
rolling a trademark along the end product—
top-quality Danish pork.*

*Arranging this apparently casual design of
metal shapes on a factory floor actually
required two full workdays and the help of a
massive overhead crane. The products are
specialty metals that meet industrial needs
with exotic materials like the cube at
the top, which measures only 15 inches on each
side but weighs 1,500 pounds.*

CO RENTMEESTER: *Pfizer annual report,* 1973

RON BARNETT: *Wallace-Murray annual report,* 1973

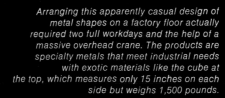

In the otherwise monochromatic setting of a Rhode Island textile factory, the photographer found a pattern of light and color in spools of yarn being fed into knitting machines. Shot from a distance and synchronized by the viewing angle, the automatic machines seem to mesh like the works of a mammoth clock.

JAY MAISEL: *Health-tex knitting plant,* 1973

... anned, but a trained eye will catch glimpses of
... lor and form that merely need to be framed
... the camera. These swirls of newly dyed carpet
... rn fell willy-nilly into a large bin, and
... e photographer shot them by available light.

ARY GLADSTONE: *HCA-Martin, Inc., annual report*, 1973

An artist-engraver, one of only nine who produce the Steuben Glass masterworks, epitomizes craftsmanship as he works an intricate, swirling design onto a $9,500 crystal sculpture.

Apparently concerned about environmentalists' opposition to Alaskan oil operations, Exxon helped to underwrite a study of the unspoiled natural life near one of its oil fields in Alaska and illustrated the study with photographs of the untrammeled wilderness nearby. This one, taken by an ornithologist, shows gulls soaring over Arctic waters.

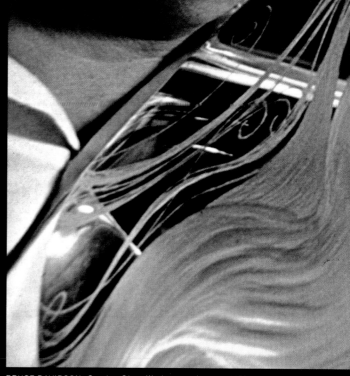

DR. GEORGE WATSON: *Exxon USA magazine*, 1973

BRUCE DAVIDSON: *Corning Glass Works annual report*, 1973

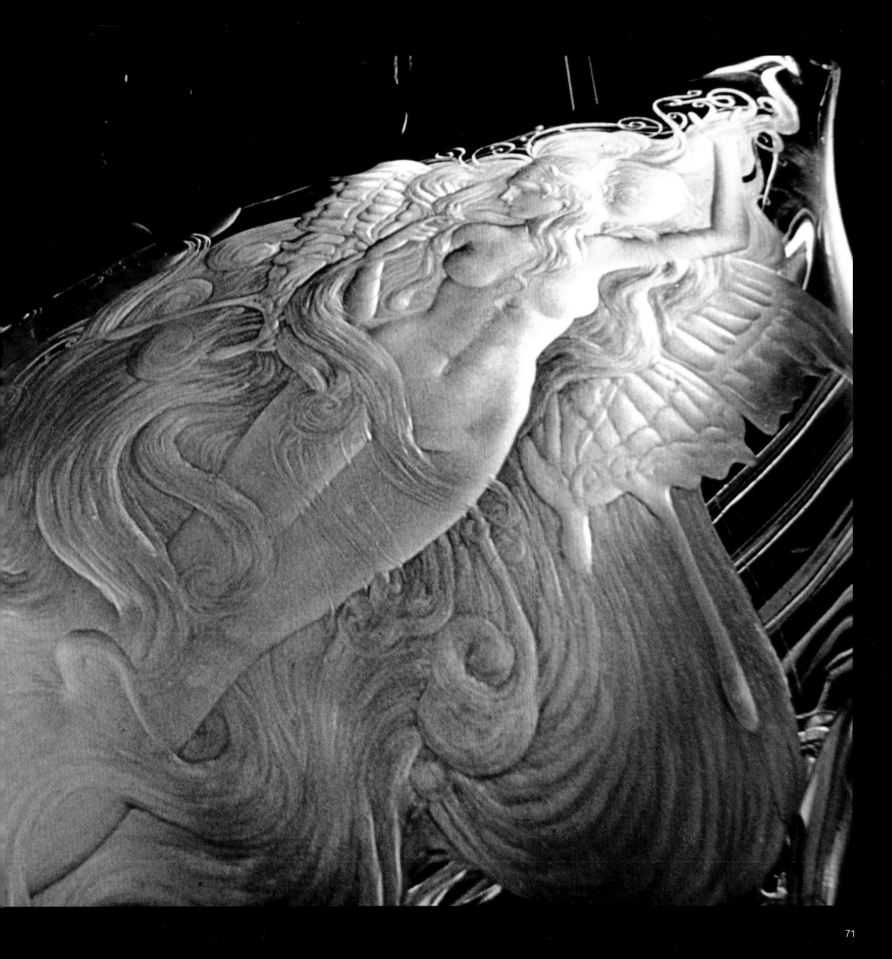

The Collecting Game

A boom in "photographica"
is shaking up the auction rooms, bringing
record prices for 19th Century prints
and such oddball antiques as cameras that
shoot through water-filled lenses

Until 1974, collecting old cameras and photographs was the cloistered pas-time of some devoted hobbyists and antique dealers. The largest price eve paid for a vintage camera at auction had been just over $2,000. But in th span of a few months this tight little world erupted as a fascinating group big-spending collectors took over. On January 24, 1974, at the famous Lor don auction gallery known as Christie's, an eccentric 19th Century came sold for $25,360. The *Times* of London dryly commented the next day: "Wit in about 150 seconds at Christie's yesterday, the value of cameras drastical changed." Twice again in London last year—once at Christie's, once Sotheby's, another large auction house—two private collectors each pa more than $25,000 for cameras almost identical to the one sold in Januar Photography was suddenly receiving unaccustomed and far-reaching atter tion—not for its technology, craft or esthetics but for the newly discovere worth of its artifacts.

Rare old photographs rose just as dizzily in value in 1974 as did the ar tique instruments that had produced them. A New York art collector pai more than $200,000 for 255 calotypes—examples of the first process to allo multiple prints from a single negative—that had been made in the 1840s b the superb Scottish portraitists David O. Hill and Robert Adamson. Just as as tonishing was the $121,000 bid by American collector Samuel Wagstaff for a album of portraits ranging from famous personalities to obscure servants b the Victorian photographer Julia Margaret Cameron. By the end of the 197 auction season Sotheby's annual photographic sales had jumped sevenfolc to $600,000. *The Wall Street Journal,* noting the significant and sudden rise i the value of vintage cameras and images, observed that "photography has good chance of following the other art markets, such as Impressionist pain ings or Pop art, right out of the realm of reality."

There seems to be no single reason behind the sudden rage for what af cionados call photographica. The gambling instinct, collectomania, person rivalry, even the state of the economy and the international money market cer tainly contribute. The international cast of collectors, who are both victim and beneficiaries of the upward spiral in value, are equally diverse: from drop out photographers to speculators, they seem to share only a belief tha photography's artifacts are worth more than a place in a museum basemen

The boom began modestly enough less than a decade ago, with a sale a the Parke Bernet auction house in New York on May 16, 1967. Will Weiss berg, the official photographer for the Waldorf Astoria Hotel in New Yor City, had died, leaving a collection of daguerreotypes, rare stereo nudes, orig inal prints by Mrs. Cameron as well as Hill and Adamson, and such equipmer as the first production-line Kodak. In a half-day sale, Parke Bernet took i $17,865. In February 1970 the same house auctioned for $61,870 the camer and photograph collection of Sidney Strober, a traveling salesman who had accumulated the objects during 20 years on the road. Dealers now agree the Strober collection would sell for at least five times as much today.

Although such an offering would fill the paneled salesrooms of London and New York with auction-goers, only a half dozen high rollers among them would be serious contenders for any valuable piece. These men are remarkable personalities—impatient to compete, skilled at the sophisticated put-ons involved in antique dealing, attracted by prizes that to ordinary folk look like junk, and rich enough to indulge a costly hobby.

When rivalry exists between two such aggressive collectors, prices skyrocket. This is exactly what happened in London with the first of the three $25,000 cameras—an English panoramic camera, designed by Thomas Sutton and produced in 1861, which takes pictures over a 120° angle. Although a rarity—there are but four known—Christie's estimated the camera would go for $2,500. The day before the sale a flurry of interest pushed the auctioneer's estimate to $7,500. But even this optimistic prediction failed to take into consideration a feud developing between Leif Preus of Norway and Michel Auer of Switzerland. At the sale, Preus and Auer bid against each other until they drove the price $15,000 beyond anything other collectors expected to spend. Preus's winning bid of $25,360 created an astonishing precedent. In March and again in April, two other Sutton cameras were sold at auction—one to Preus, the other to Anthony Wigram, a London businessman somewhat new to camera collecting—for even higher figures.

Preus, who operates a photo-finishing company in his native city of Horten, 60 miles south of Oslo, intends to place the two Suttons in his own photographic museum. "My object," he says, "has never been to make money on the items. Nor have I wanted to collect cameras just to put them away in big boxes." Recalling the origin of his fascination with old equipment, he explains, "One day I was given a Hasselblad Svenska Express, a camera that had been made in Italy but sold by Hasselblad in Sweden. I studied the camera, and my interest began to grow." Preus has since bought more than 500 cameras, 75 of which he labels significant.

The other side of the bidding duel for the Sutton camera, Michel Auer, came to collecting by a different route. Now the owner of a company in Geneva that makes photographic murals, he earlier had gained practical respect for the camera as a fashion photographer. But once his collecting days began a dozen years ago, this respect developed into a determination to document as completely as possible the history of camera technology, and he has amassed probably the largest and most valuable private camera collection in the world. A few years ago he sold many of his antiques to the Sterckshof Museum in Antwerp, but he continues to pursue the pieces—such as the Sutton—that will fill out the gaps in his collection. Auer routinely flies to Paris, London—or Columbus, Ohio—if he senses an important discovery. Sotheby's one day, the Ohio Camera Collectors Society the next.

Auer lost out on the three Sutton cameras when the bidding exceeded the limits even he imagined possible. "I was right beside Michel at the third Sutton auction," says Matthew Isenberg, a Connecticut car dealer who has accumulated one of the largest private collections in the United States, some of it by telephone from his backyard swimming pool. "When the bidding for the Sutton got close to $25,000, Michel said, 'This is insane,' and got out."

Isenberg chose to collect cameras instead of photographs with an eye on the championship: "Why should I want to be 19th in images when I can be the king of hardware?" He started out by concentrating on Leicas. The Leica collectors have their own national organization, publish a small newsletter and hold their own conventions and meetings. Each member hopes to own every model ever manufactured—but particularly the elusive Model B, of which fewer than 1,200 were made, all between 1926 and 1931. At the Columbus fair in May 1974, Isenberg paid $2,500 for a Model B. But now he specializes in what he calls "early and landmark stuff, the first-of-a-kind item every true collector dreams of having." The living room in his home contains a half dozen shiny daguerreotype cameras, several of them on tripods like splendid pieces of antique furniture. "Everything you see here is a Mona Lisa," he says, mixing his images.

If the appearance of a Sutton camera was enough to produce a tempest in London auction houses, an even greater reaction would be stirred by the first commercial daguerreotype camera. Isenberg calls such a camera—manufactured by Alphonse Giroux, Daguerre's brother-in-law—"the absolute pinnacle. One would sell for $50,000 to $100,000."

Just as Daguerre's own camera would cause equipment collectors to run for their checkbooks, certain products of such a camera stimulate extravagance among "image collectors," a related but separate breed, who buy old photographs. The ultimate prize they hunt is a series of 300 daguerreotypes of the American West taken by Robert H. Vance in the 1840s and '50s, including many chronicling the Gold Rush of 1849. They have been lost for almost a century. Vance exhibited the scenes in city after city until somewhere—presumably in the Middle West—the pictures disappeared.

If the Vance daguerreotypes are ever found, they are likely to end up in the hands of George Rinhart, a 30-year-old New York photographic dealer, or Arnold Crane, a Chicago lawyer who is Rinhart's best customer. Unlike camera competitors Preus and Auer, Rinhart and Crane often collaborate in tracking and successfully bidding for valuable finds.

Rinhart, who transacts business from his terraced apartment on Park Avenue, trades heavily on his thorough knowledge of photographic history. At a 1970 New York auction fair, he recognized some old portraits to be close-ups of the Lincoln assassination conspirators taken by Civil War photographer Alexander Gardner. In Vermont, Rinhart came across twelve albums that turned out to be volumes of rare 19th Century American photographs, including a calotype of Millard Fillmore, 13th president of the United States.

Such finds have served Rinhart in helping Arnold Crane to gather the largest and most impressive private collection of photographic prints in the world. "He is as intense as any man I've met," Rinhart says of Crane with the enthusiasm typical of those possessed by collecting. "He had the courage to start buying eight years ago, before anyone cared—the Dark Ages in this business. It was like collecting a Renoir in 1875." But whereas camera collector Isenberg surrounds himself with his "Mona Lisas," print collector Crane must keep his "Renoirs" in a vault to protect their fragile beauty.

Among Crane's treasures is an album by the French photographic pioneer Hippolyte Bayard, now worth perhaps $500,000. The escalation that leads to such valuations is illustrated by a three-way transaction beginning with Rinhart and ending in Crane's vault. Rinhart bought a daguerreotype of Edgar Allen Poe made in 1848, a year before the author's death, for $9,250 at an auction in Chicago. He immediately sold it for $18,750 to the Scott Elliott Gallery of New York, which in turn sold it to Crane for $38,000, the highest price yet paid for a single photograph.

Not all passionate collectors, however, need the resources of Crane or Auer. Knowledge of photographic history, time to scour local markets, and a certain steadiness of the nerves can bring a collecting victory—or a bust. Mike Kessler, a young Southern California collector, managed both with the same item. Kessler crisscrosses the country, bartering, buying and selling until he has the pieces he wants. His biggest find was a group of seven daguerreotypes taken in Washington, D.C. about 1846, including some of the first known photographs of the Capitol and the White House.

Kessler came upon the daguerreotypes at the same time another California collector, Larry Shirer, spotted them at a flea market outside San Francisco. Each bought a few. But later Kessler, nudged, he says, by intuition and a desire to own the complete set, approached Shirer and offered him $300 worth of equipment in trade for his pictures. Nine months later Kessler sold six of the seven to the Library of Congress for $12,000. Shirer is philosophical about the deal. "Mike may be a shark and I may be a mark," he observed, "but look at it this way: I paid $22 for the stuff and got $300 in return. He got $12,000, but if he had waited a few years he could have made six or seven times as much."

Soaring Bids for Antique Hardware

The prices of 19th Century cameras were pushed to record highs in 1974 by competition for what collectors believed were unique models. Ironically, in spite of the discovery of duplicates for some models, auction prices increased.

Until this year, photographic historians thought that the only surviving 1861 Sutton panoramic camera was owned by the Royal Photographic Society in London. When a second one turned up at auction in January 1974, the scramble for the camera drove the price to $25,360. Then two additional specimens appeared at auction during the year —and surprisingly, the prices rose with each sale. It turned out that Suttons are prized not only for their rarity, but also as the oldest existing examples of panoramic cameras—the surviving relics of an era when landscape photography grappled with the optical problem of capturing without distortion a breadth of view as wide as the one encompassed by the human eye.

While panoramic cameras fascinate some collectors, other enthusiasts compete for early stereoscopic cameras like the French Koch camera on page 79. Still another coveted antique is the Stirn *(page 78),* a detective camera that could be concealed beneath a vest. In the 1890s, one anonymous photographer used such a camera to make early documentary pictures of the sordid conditions inside a women's prison in England.

Anthony Wigram paid $26,565 for this Sutton camera in April 1974. Its lens, a thick-walled water-filled sphere, projects a 120° image upon a glass plate, curved to keep everything in focus from edge to edge. The plate is housed in the detachable holder at the right.

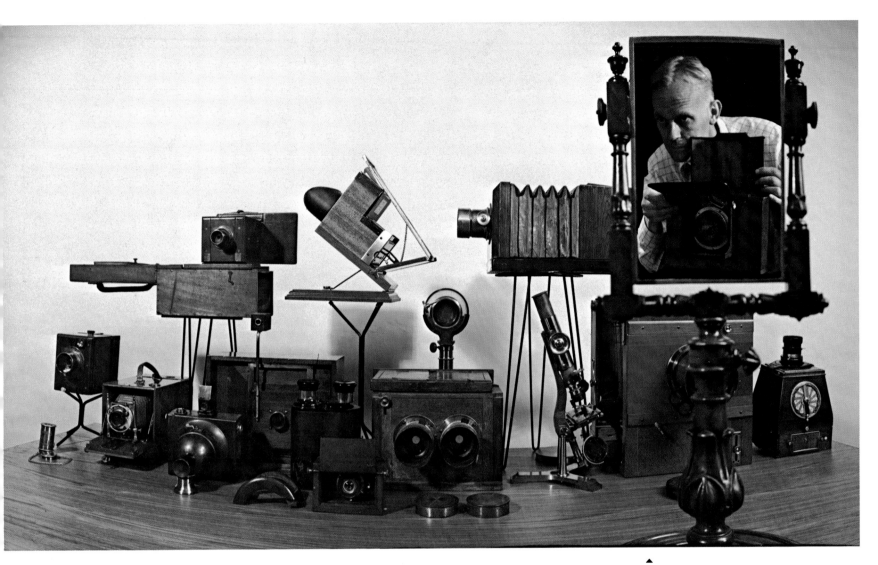

Camera collector Leif Preus photographed himself in a mirror using the $25,360 Thomas Sutton panoramic camera he purchased in 1974. For the photograph, Preus assembled the prizes of his 700 piece collection of cameras, microscopic viewers, light meters and other optical instruments. Near the center of the table, just to the left of a two-lens stereo camera, stands a second, smaller panoramic camera by Sutton that Preus bought in 1974. A rare American daguerreotype camera stands to the left of the mirror. The French Sigriste at far right, made in 1900, is capable of shutter speeds of up to 1/10,000 of a second.

Anthony Wigram got a bonus of seven exposed negatives when he bought his Sutton. The positive at left, made for this book, was printed in a rounded holder built to protect the curved glass negative. It shows a view of Gibraltar which, judging from the type of musket carried by the British soldiers, was made about 1865.

Collectors consider this rare C. P. Stirn Patent Concealed Vest Camera well worth the $1,500 it brought at auction last year. The center knob rotated a circular film plate and cocked the shutter to make a total of four photographs.

This 1857 Koch stereoscopic camera, which brought $3,400 at auction, is an early example of fine workmanship—Koch, who made the body, was trained as a cabinetmaker. The buyer, Matthew Isenberg, knows of no other camera exactly like it, but its high sale price increases the likelihood that if another does exist it will soon appear on the market.

A Scramble for Old Photographs

In 1974 the values of antique prints virtually exploded. When an album of 94 portraits by Victorian photographer Julia Margaret Cameron was auctioned off in London, the winning bid of $121,000 set an auction record for a single lot of 19th Century prints. Dealers attribute the boom in Cameron prices to deliberate attempts to corner a small supply: Julia Cameron took her first photograph in her late forties, and did her best work in barely a dozen years.

Far more prolific was the partnership of two Scotsmen, David Octavius Hill and Robert Adamson, who produced some of the Victorian era's best outdoor portraits. But since their work seldom changes hands, in 1974 a set of 255 prints was snapped up for over $200,000.

The work of American photographers also brought record prices. In 1866, when Alexander Gardner offered a $150 two-volume documentation of the Civil War to a war-weary American public, he found few takers. In June 1974, however, a first volume from one of the rare sets sold to New York dealer Janet Lehr for $8,000.

Alexander Gardner's son James took this picture—one of 50 in the first volume of Gardner's "Photographic Sketch Book of The War"—of a church of the Dunker sect on the Antietam battlefield in Maryland. Fierce fighting swept around the church during the battle.

JAMES GARDNER: *Dunker church, battlefield of Antietam, Maryland, 1862*

Ponderous siege cannons, which could hurl 100-pound shot at a target three miles away, routed the Confederates at Yorktown, Virginia, in 1862. The Photographic Sketch Book contained 83 pictures by photographers other than Gardner, though he made all the prints himself.

WOOD and GIBSON: *Battery No. 1, near Yorktown, Virginia,* 1862

Pausing as if on a peacetime stroll, a civilian surveys the shell-torn desolation of the navy yard at Norfolk, Virginia. In 1864, when James Gardner took the picture, the navy yard—twice destroyed, by the retreating armies of both sides—was being rebuilt to service the steamers docked at right.

JAMES GARDNER: *Ruins of Norfolk Navy Yard, Virginia,* 1864

Four portraits and figure studies by Julia Margaret Cameron, from an album of 94 prints auctioned in the fall of 1974 for $121,000, illustrate her bold, sometimes eccentric, always intensely personal style. Mrs. Cameron's subjects had to hold stiff poses during exposures lasting as long as seven minutes. Processing her prints in a tiny lab, she refused to remove dust spots and smears because she considered them visible evidence of her creative struggle.

G. F. Watts, c. 1867

Freddy Gould and Lizzie Koewen, 1865

Mary Hillier with Two Children, 1864

Alfred Tennyson, c. 1867

Miss Murray

William Leighton Leitch

Bonaly Tower

John Brown, M.D.

Photography as a practicable art was scarcely five years old in 1843 when David O. Hill and Robert Adamson began to produce calotypes like these. Introduced in 1840, the calotype process was the first to provide re-usable paper negatives from which multiple prints could be made.

The New Technology/3

The New Technology/3

A radically new lens is drawn automatically by a plotting device linked to an IBM 370 computer. With a 228mm f/1.5 lens similar in design, amateur photographers may someday take high-speed pictures by starlight—but at present, computers are speeding the design of such lenses solely for military use.

The New Optics/ ENRICO FERORELLI: *A new lens design print-out in the computer room of an optical manufacturer*

Innovations in Lens Design

Computers and coating techniques are producing superb new lenses: smaller, lighter and sharper

An array of lenses never before available—astonishingly faster, sharper and smaller than their older counterparts—appeared this year, largely as a result of two technological innovations. A process called multi-layer lens coating virtually eliminates glare and reflections from lens surfaces, and makes certain special-purpose designs, particularly for multi-element zoom lenses, commercially practical. An effective wide-angle zoom lens would not even be possible without multi-layer coating; with the coating commercially available, the year 1974 saw the introduction of a 28mm-45mm zoom lens (page 93) that promises the sharpness and resolution of a fixed-focal-length lens. The second, equally important development is the expanding role of computers in calculating lens designs. Computers have reduced dramatically the time needed to develop new lenses, mainly through their ability to handle at lightning speed the mathematical computations essential to modern lens design. The result has been more efficient lenses—and some unusual lenses that would not have seemed practicable only a few years ago.

The benefits provided by computers and multi-layer coating are closely interrelated. As it happens, multi-layer coating calls for an especially large number of calculations, and the computer handles them easily. But multi-layer coating itself is really an extension of an existing process. Lenses have long been coated with one, two, or three layers of anti-reflective material. Multi-layer coating is the application of more than three coats. Additional layers cut down the amount of light lost to reflection, though at a price in dollars: the six to 11 coated layers incorporated in most of the new lenses add from 15 to 20 per cent to the cost of manufacture.

The coatings are needed because a beam of light does not pass completely through a piece of glass. Anyone who has seen his own image as he looks into a shop window knows that some light is always reflected back by a glass surface. Camera lenses are made of many individual pieces of optical glass, technically called elements. As light passes through each element, it strikes two separate air-to-glass surfaces, one as it enters, another as it leaves. At an uncoated surface, the rays lose from four to eight per cent of their light to reflection. In a single-element lens this loss is negligible. But in a multi-element lens the light losses add up. An uncoated 135mm lens for a 35mm camera, which can do its job with four elements, may give up more than a quarter of its light to reflection. A 54mm-270mm zoom lens, with as many as 15 elements, loses well over half its light.

To make matters worse, this reflected light does not conveniently drift off into thin air. Trapped inside the lens, it bounces between elements, throws a contrast-reducing haze across the entire picture, and mars the image with blots of light. These reflection problems become most acute when the camera is aimed directly at a light source (page 91).

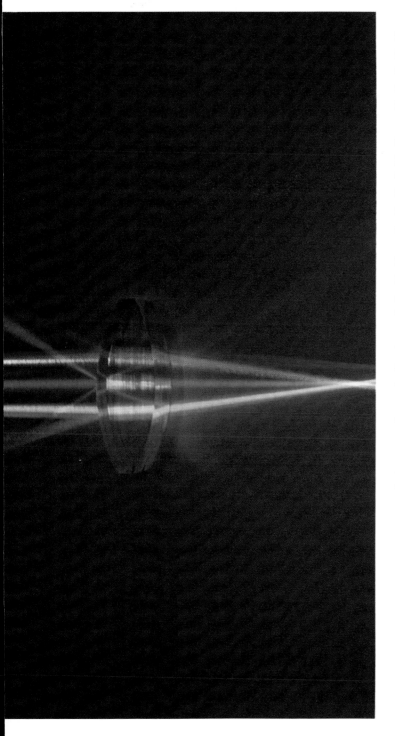

About four per cent of the light striking an uncoated plastic lens (below) bounces off its surface because of the difference between the speed of light in the surrounding air and the speed of light in the plastic of the lens. Some reflected rays of light eventually show up on the film as diffused haze or splotches.

Anti-reflective lens coatings are made of such compounds as magnesium fluoride or zirconium oxide. These substances adhere to glass; they absorb almost no light; they do not shrivel or crack under the heat of the sun, freeze or flake in cold air, or wash away in the rain. Their primary qualification as coating materials, however, is that they can be deposited in uniform, sub-microscopically thin, precisely controlled layers.

A second requirement satisfied by these chemicals is the speed of light inside them—indicated by a measure called the refractive index; it too must be precisely controlled. Taken together, the refractive index and the thickness of a coating determine the time a light wave takes to travel through the coating; this time, in turn, determines what happens to reflections. When a coating has the right refractive index and the right thickness, reflections are reduced and the energy of their light is transmitted through the lens *(page 91)*.

The coating accomplishes this extraordinary transformation by forming two separate waves of reflected light. The first wave is reflected when rays of light hit the outer surface of the coating; most of the rays pass through, but some bounce back. The rays that continue through the coating strike the surface of the glass; there, a few more bounce back to form the second wave.

The relationship between these two reflected waves is crucial. It is determined by the distance the original light waves travel between the outer and inner surfaces of the coating. Ideally this distance must be one quarter of the wavelength of the light. The part of the light that strikes the glass and rebounds back through the coating then travels another quarter wavelength —in all, one half of its wavelength. When the second reflected wave passes back through the coating, it is out of step with the first reflected wave because it has traveled half a wavelength farther. The high point, or crest, of one wave meets the low point, or trough, of the other, and in this crest-to-trough interaction, the two waves cancel each other out.

The light has not been eliminated—light is a form of energy and energy cannot be destroyed. But instead of bouncing around as reflections, the energy of the reflected light is incorporated with the beam of transmitted light that passes all the way through the lens. In simplified terms, the light that would have been lost to reflection in an uncoated lens passes through the coated glass to reach the film, reinforcing the original, unreflected waves that passed straight through. The haze is eliminated; there are no blots of light—and since more light gets to the film, the effective speed of the lens is increased.

Because every color in the spectrum of visible light has a different wavelength, a single coating can reduce reflections to a minimum over a small range of colors. Violet light has a wavelength of about .4 micron (16 millionths of an inch); the wavelength of red light, at the opposite end of the spectrum, is about .65 micron (25 millionths of an inch). For a typical coating material, a layer about .1 micron thick will be one quarter of the wavelength of violet light, while for red light the coating must be about .12 micron in thickness. Other coatings, of different thicknesses, will reduce reflections of the other colors.

By stacking up six or seven coatings of different thicknesses, about 95 per cent of all the wavelengths in the spectrum can be accounted for. Together, the stack of multi-layer coated elements allows almost every color to pass through the complete camera lens with little reflected light. Reflection is reduced to an inconsequential .4 per cent at every coated-glass surface.

The precise array of perfect coatings calls for manufacturing to fantastically close tolerances. Nowadays, lens coating is performed in a huge metal chamber outfitted with a vacuum pump and electric heaters. At the bottom of the chamber, crucibles hold the powdered coating materials. The lenses—as many as 250 in one batch—are lined up in a rack set in the chamber. The chamber is sealed and the pump exhausts its air. Then the lenses and the crucible containing the first coating material are heated. The powder melts, the crucible cover is mechanically opened, and the molecules rise as a vapor in a thin, uniform cloud. The molecules of vaporized material condense onto the hot surfaces of the lenses and are baked in place. As the molecules gather on the lens surfaces, the light transmitted through one of the lenses is measured by a sensing device that indicates the thickness of the coating. When the coating reaches the correct thickness, the process is stopped almost instantaneously.

For each additional coating the process is repeated, using successive crucibles of material. Since the coatings must interact to cover as much of the spectrum as possible, the precision of each individual coating is an important factor in the design and the performance of the lens.

Before computers lightened the load, almost all aspects of lens design were tedious exercises in mathematical computation, with a lot of trial and error thrown in. The trial and error still exists, but with computers speeding the calculations, lens designers are freer to indulge their creativity.

Suppose a manufacturer decides that there is an attractive potential market for a lens that will photograph distant objects under low-available-light conditions. A designer starts with the specifications of an established lens design that most nearly matches the one he wants to make. In this case, he might use a 200mm f/4.5 lens, knowing that he must redesign it for a larger aperture—f/2.8—to allow more light to enter.

The specifications of the existing lens are programed in a computer; they include such data as the refractive index and dispersion qualities of the glass, the thickness of each element and the distances between the elements. Relying on his experience, the designer alters these variables in the computer.

A diagram shows how coatings cancel out most reflections. As the light wave moves from the air through a single coating, it slows down; it changes speed again as it reaches the glass. At each of these boundaries, a part of the light wave is reflected. The lens coating makes the light bounce in a predetermined way.

The reflection from the air-to-coating boundary is exactly half a wavelength ahead of that from the coating-to-glass boundary. The crest of the first wave and the trough of the second cancel each other out, an effect symbolized by the fading red lines. Most of the light, no longer bouncing about, now passes through the coating and lens.

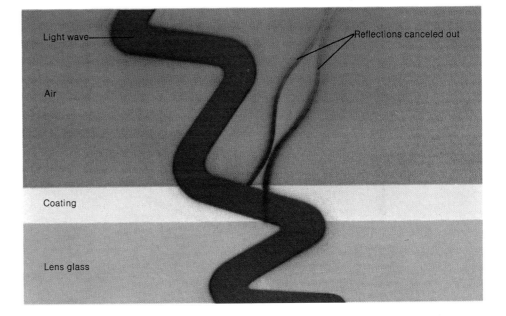

A photograph shot into a low-lying afternoon sun (top picture) with a conventionally coated lens is marred by flare (the light haze) and ghosts (the yellow blots) in the lower center, caused by reflected light bouncing around inside the lens. The same picture shot 15 seconds later at the same exposure setting but with a lens containing seven layers of anti-reflective coating is clear of flare and ghosts (bottom picture).

He may change the spaces between elements, for example, or try elements of different thicknesses; in effect, he experiments by computer to rearrange the old design to fit the new requirements.

Each tentative new version of the lens is evaluated mathematically by tracing simulated rays of light through simulated glass elements and air spaces to the spot where they would strike the film plane. If a ray hits the plane off the mark—an event that the designer can detect from a computer print-out—the aberrations of the hypothetical lens must be corrected. The variables are changed and evaluated repeatedly, until the desired result is achieved.

Using a desk calculator, a designer can trace a single ray through a projected new lens arrangement in about an hour: the computer does it in 1/100 of a second. Plotting the thousands of rays that bombard a lens from every angle would occupy a calculator-equipped designer for years; the computer completes the job in minutes. Because of its lightning-quick ability to do the math, the computer gives the designer freedom to attempt hundreds of variations of a lens design. And until all these variables have been evaluated by the computer, there is no need to grind, coat, or assemble a lens.

Because of the efficient design of the resulting new lens, it may require one less element, or a smaller distance between elements, than any earlier but otherwise equivalent lens. In this case, photographers would be getting a more compact lens than ever before—thanks to the new design opportunities made possible by the aid of the computer.

Exotic but Practical Lenses

The largest and most innovative collection of new lenses in years was introduced to the market in 1974—a generation of lenses produced by radically new techniques of commercial design and development *(pages 88 to 91)*. Most of these lenses are as practical as they are exotic in design. Almost all of them are so expensive—even when mass produced—that few photographers can afford to adopt them as standard equipment. But every professional and advanced amateur will be fascinated by their construction and special features. The five pictured on these pages include a mass-produced aspherical lens, for sharp images at large apertures; a variable-field-curvature lens that provides unprecedented control over focus; a compact telephoto; a fisheye; and a zoom.

A Cheaper Aspherical

Camera manufacturers have been experimenting with aspherical lenses for more than a decade, simply because an aspherical lens virtually eliminates flare, and it provides a sharper image at large-aperture settings than a spherical lens does. The light rays that pass through the edge of an ordinary spherical lens at large apertures bend so much that they focus at a different point from rays passing through the center of the lens, thus creating a blurred image on the film. An aspherical design solves the problem with a lens that has one curve near the edge and another at the center.

Before 1974 aspherical lenses had to be produced by hand because of their complexity of design. Now for the first time Canon is mass-producing multi-layer coated asphericals designed with the aid of computers. The manufacturer offers a range of these lenses—24mm, 55mm and 85mm—all priced significantly lower than handmade models; the 85mm lens is the fastest medium telephoto lens for 35mm SLRs now on the market.

A Canon 85mm f/1.2 aspherical lens

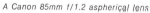

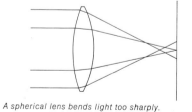

A spherical lens bends light too sharply.

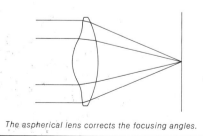

The aspherical lens corrects the focusing angles.

Flexible Fields of Focus

By adjusting a control ring on the barrel of the Minolta variable-field-curvature lens, a photographer can focus the edges of an image separately from the center. Shooting a deeply recessed three-dimensional subject, a photographer using ordinary lenses must stop his lens down to increase depth of field—with a resulting loss of speed. With the compact Minolta lens—only two inches long and weighing just over 12 ounces—the photographer can focus sharply all the points on a concave or a convex subject by simply moving the ring.

The Minolta 24mm f/2.8 variable-field curvature

A Shorter Telescopic Lens

A 600mm telephoto lens usually extends to a clumsy 20 inches. Vivitar has drastically reduced this problem using a system of mirrors that reflect the light rays and make them travel farther. This new lens takes a further step with the use of solid glass, virtually eliminating the air space inside the lens. The result is a telescopic lens that is not only sturdier but far smaller than any oth-

The Vivitar 600mm f/8 solid catadioptric

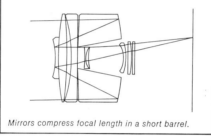

Mirrors compress focal length in a short barrel.

er: only 4.2 inches. Appropriately, the new lens got its first workout in the cramped environment of spacecraft observatories.

An Improved Fisheye

The extreme curvature of a complex fisheye lens enables a camera to survey a field of vision 180° wide, creating some of the most dramatic images in all photography. But the same curvature also creates prob-

The Olympus Zuiko fisheye 16mm f/3.5

lems: bending light at very sharp angles produces aberrations, especially in close-ups. Olympus put its computers to work recalculating the fisheye's curves and came up with a remarkable lens that includes 11 elements of optical glass designed to correct these aberrations—all compressed into a 1 1/10-inch barrel that weighs only 6 ounces. The new fisheye is capable of producing sharply defined pictures at focuses from eight inches to infinity.

A Sharp, All-Purpose Zoom

Zoom-lens photographs are generally less crisp than those taken with individual fixed-focal-length lenses, but multi-layer coating in the zoom can narrow or even eliminate the gap in quality. Nikkor's designers have combined 11 elements, most multi-layer coated, to produce a lens able to make sharp images over

The Nikkor 28mm-45mm f/4.5 zoom

a shooting range that starts at 24 inches. And because it can be set for either wide-angle or normal pictures, the new lens is not only accurate but versatile as well.

A Crisis in Silver

An intense, secrecy-shrouded search for alternatives to current light-sensitive compounds is turning up some real possibilities—but they are probably far off in the future

In a year when a great many basics that are normally taken for granted turned up scarce, expensive, or damaging to the environment, photographers could not expect to be spared—and they weren't. In fact, the very foundation of photography developed these alarming drawbacks.

Photography is based on one substance: silver. In nearly all photographic films and papers its compounds make the picture. And now silver is not only in great demand, and thus expensive, but the chemicals needed to process silver-based photographic supplies have been found to be pollutants. The situation became grave enough in 1974 to pose the problems: Can silver survive as a basic material of photography? If not, are there any materials that can replace it?

All commonly used photographic films and papers are coated with microscopic crystals of silver bromide, silver chloride or silver iodide (or mixtures) suspended in a transparent gelatin made from animal hides and bones. In the year 1973, for example, photographic products contained 50 million troy ounces of silver (the troy ounce, used for precious stones and metals, equals 1.1 avoirdupois ounce), about a quarter of the total U.S. consumption of the metal.

Obviously the price of silver affects the price of a roll of film or a package of paper, and the price of silver is rapidly rising. Rarely more than $2.00 an ounce before 1973, it streaked to a record $6.70 an ounce in the first months of 1974. Such peaks may be short lived, but the general price trend is clear: both silver and the photographic products that are made from it are going to cost much more in the years ahead.

Pollution is a further problem. When black and white film is developed, silver compounds that have been exposed to light form metallic silver in a photographic image; when the image is fixed, the unexposed silver compounds are washed away. In color-film processing all of the silver is dissolved into the fixer bath, because a final color image is composed not of silver but of dyes. Most commercial processors reclaim the silver dissolved in the fixer (it is too costly to throw away), but the chemicals used to process films and prints go down the drain to pollute rivers and streams. These chemical pollutants have become an environmental problem. In 1974, the United States government imposed a timetable of strict regulations on commercial photographic processors to force them to clean up their wastes. Eventually, the cost of this clean-up will be passed along to the consumer in increased processing charges—to add to the rising cost of silver.

For more than 25 years, world-wide consumption of silver has exceeded the output of the world's silver mines. To help fill this gap, millions of ounces of silver have been retrieved and recycled in the United States in recent years.

As their raw material, the recyclers collect battered silverware, old X-ray films, used photographic chemicals—even old silver coins. (Silver is now simply too expensive for most governments, including that of the United States, to use for their coinage; since 1965, for example, American "silver" quarters and dimes have actually been made of a mixture of cheaper metals —nickel and copper.)

But much silver remains unavailable for recycling. Vast amounts of silver now go into commemorative coins, ingots and medals, where they generally stay. Commemorative collecting was once the preserve of a few hobbyists, but now it is big business; in 1973, it gobbled up 23 million ounces of silver for such memorabilia as sets of ingots "honoring the greatest cars of the automobile's first hundred years."

Commemoratives are rarely recycled; instead, they are held by collectors who hope that prices will rise. Large-scale speculation in the raw metal also goes on. In London, New York and Chicago, investors buy and hold title to enormous amounts of silver, much as investors hold stocks or bonds for increase in value. One private speculator in silver is rumored to own over 20 million ounces.

Manufacturers of photographic supplies, faced by the competing demands of commemorative-makers, speculators, and such industries as electronics, have been looking for practical alternatives to silver. In the hunt for non-silver processes, old discoveries are being re-examined and new approaches are being developed. The hunt is intense, involving research expenditures in the millions of dollars. It is also secretive. But one outcome is becoming unhappily clear. None of the non-silver processes now under investigation is as sensitive to light as silver is.

Silver and photography have been synonymous since photography was invented because silver has an especially useful form of "light sensitivity" (the term scientists use to describe any reaction that takes place when a substance is exposed to light). Compounds of silver with iodine, bromine or chlorine—known collectively as silver halides—produce a detectable reaction even when exposed to incredibly small amounts of light. When a silver halide crystal is struck by as few as four photons of light (a flashlight bulb emits a million billion photons per second), a few atoms of the exposed crystal change into metallic silver. That is enough to make the entire exposed crystal—billions of atoms—become metallic silver in the developing tank, and thus build up a silver image. The areas struck by the most light are blackened by metallic silver; areas that are not struck by light remain transparent after processing, because no silver has been built up. Between these extremes, intermediate areas have varying amounts of silver, creating shades of gray. This range from black through shades of gray to white, generated by varying amounts of silver metal, enables silver-based photography to reproduce the subtle tones and fine detail of a scene. The fact that silver can do this after a split-second exposure to light explains its essential role in photography.

At present no non-silver process combines these virtues of fast, efficient reaction and excellent tonal reproduction. But four alternatives currently being studied are the vesicular, the photopolymer, the developable-free-radical, and the electrostatic processes. All four are potentially cheaper and cleaner than silver. As yet, none is as light sensitive, but each has already proved practical for limited purposes.

The vesicular process, used to make copies of motion-picture film and microfilms of printed documents, is based on a complex, light-sensitive molecule called a diazonium compound, which is embedded in a plastic material. When the diazonium molecule is exposed to light it breaks up, releasing atoms of nitrogen gas. Before the nitrogen atoms can escape into the atmosphere, however, the film is heated; under the heat the gas expands to form bubble-like cavities, called vesicles, in the plastic, and this pattern of vesicles forms the image. A second exposure to light destroys the remaining light-sensitive molecules. Commercially available vesicular films are not sensitive to visible light; they respond instead to ultraviolet rays, and are therefore useless for ordinary photography. But the Kalvar Corporation of New Orleans has produced an experimental emulsion sensitive to the green component of ordinary light, and research along these lines is continuing. Since applications of heat, rather than baths of water and chemicals, are used to process vesicular film, it is a cleaner process than silver. The U.S. Navy is considering vesicular film for use on board ships, where the problems posed by wastes, special plumbing requirements and the need to

Bubbles in Plastic

Vesicular film uses light-sensitive molecules embedded in a plastic coating. When exposed to light (left), the molecules break up, releasing atoms of nitrogen gas. Before the atoms can escape into the atmosphere, the film is heated (below). The gas expands, forming an image made up of bubble-like cavities, or vesicles, in the plastic, which hardens around them. A second exposure to light—but not to heat—fixes the negative bubble image by breaking up remaining sensitive molecules and allowing the nitrogen gas to escape.

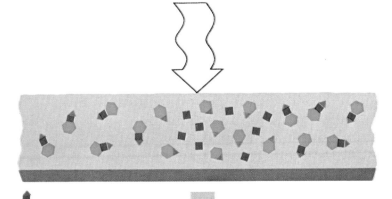

Light-sensitive molecule ■ Nitrogen ▪ Plastic

conserve supplies of fresh water combine to make silver-based photography especially inconvenient.

In the photopolymer process, exposure to light triggers the rapid organization of a group of relatively simple molecules, or monomers, into long molecular chains called polymers. The monomers in unexposed areas can be washed away by a solvent, leaving the polymer chains standing out in low relief, and the image formed by these clusters of polymers can be dyed for viewing or inked for printing. Polymer images are generally restricted to stark black and white, but Du Pont is working on a coating that will record the full tonal range required for general photography. Although photopolymer film is 10,000 times faster—that is, more light sensitive—than vesicular film, it still needs 100,000 times more light than silver does.

A third possible alternative to silver is developable-free-radical film, which is coated with a solution of complex light-sensitive molecules. When exposed to blue light, some of these molecules break apart, forming a visible dye. The dye from the blue-light exposure makes the coating sensitive to another color of light, used in processing. When the film is flooded with such light, additional dye molecules are formed adjacent to the first, intensifying the image. Since the dye molecules are smaller than the metallic grains that form an image on silver-based film, a free-radical film can record greater detail. This experimental film, now being refined by Horizons Incorporated, of Cleveland, Ohio, is approaching the minimal speed needed for camera use. The U.S. Air Force is studying its application to aerial photography, since free-radical film would show far more ground detail than is now possible with silver film. As a result of the military interest in this type, many of the new findings on free-radical film are classified.

Chains of Molecules

In the photopolymer process, exposure to light causes relatively small molecules called monomers to form long chains of molecules called polymers. The process begins when light disrupts an "initiator," allowing it to hook onto a nearby monomer. That one hooks onto another, and so on, in a chain reaction (below) that brings many neighboring monomers into a network of interlocking polymers. Washing with a solvent (right) removes monomers from unexposed areas, leaving a pattern of polymers to form the negative image.

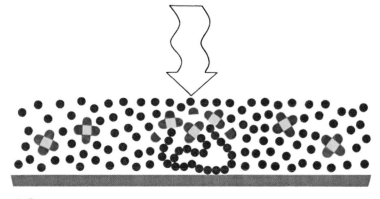

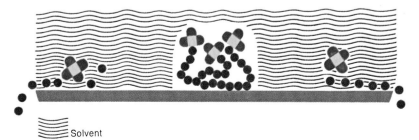

Initiator ●Monomer

≈≈≈Solvent

The fourth non-silver process is already in common use in office copying-machines. It is xerography, in which images are formed by electrostatic charges. A camera based on the process would first deposit a pattern of electric charges on a transparent film coating. Then an exposure could be made. Wherever light struck the film, the charge would be neutralized, leaving a pattern of charges corresponding to an image on the film. Oppositely charged particles of colored "toner," spread over the film, would then adhere in this pattern, because opposite charges attract; when heated, the particles would fuse to fix the image. In a recent experiment Scott Graphics, of Holyoke, Massachusetts, successfully used xerographic film in an ordinary camera; in daylight, an exposure of 10 seconds at f/8 produced a good image.

Like the other three alternatives to silver, xerography is practical for certain limited reproduction purposes, but, like the others, it does not yet combine silver's speed with its subtlety of tones and detail. Countering this deficiency is the ecological advantage that all four alternatives share over silver. The fact that they are less polluting could prove crucial, for of all the threats to silver-based photography, pollution is perhaps the most serious.

The pollution problem commands international attention, and its solution is bound to be costly, tightening the economic squeeze applied by soaring silver prices. But even if silver prices can be lowered, silver-based photography may have to be replaced simply because the chemicals involved in it are so dirty. The pollution they create, like that from other industrial wastes, is being strictly regulated by the United States Environmental Protection Agency; to meet the new requirements, photofinishers will have to treat their wastes before disposing of them, and some may have to build entire sewage treat-

Formation of Dyes

The developable free radical type of film is coated with a solution of complex molecules sensitive to blue light, or to the blue component of multicolored light. When struck by such light, this kind of molecule breaks apart (left), and one fragment forms a visible dye. The dye makes unfragmented molecules react when the film is struck by light of a different color. Overall exposure to this second color causes molecules adjacent to the dye to break up as well (below), increasing the density of the image. Heat destroys any remaining light-sensitive molecules.

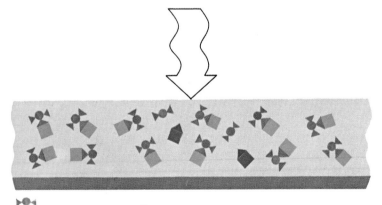

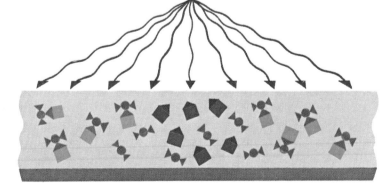

◄●► Light-sensitive molecule ▲ Dye

ment plants similar to, but smaller than, those needed to treat the wastes of cities. The cost of such plants is, of course, enormous.

One approach to the pollution problem has been to improve the chemical make-up of the processing solutions. To eliminate harmful amounts of zinc, formaldehyde and other chemicals, Eastman Kodak began in 1972 to introduce new processing solutions for color films, and new films and papers to go with this new chemistry. The new, Kodak-formulated chemicals will process the great bulk of all the pictures taken in the United States. Although this new chemistry requires new and expensive equipment, the cost should be made up in the long run by greater efficiency. Less time is needed to produce a finished picture, and the chemicals are more easily rejuvenated and re-used than in the old systems.

Part of the recycling encouraged by the new system involves recovering the silver dissolved in the solutions, and large processors have been getting hundreds of thousands of dollars worth of silver yearly from fixers. The new bleach-fix can not only be mined for this silver but conveniently re-used, reducing the amount of wastes the processor and the environment must contend with. As a result, many small processors who have been neither recovering nor recycling are now finding it profitable to do so.

By all these methods the world of photography is trying to substitute for and save its precious metal. But unless prices go down and the pollution problem is solved, silver's permanent use in photography remains in peril. Although no non-silver process can yet compete with silver, it is more than likely that a photographer of the 21st Century will be using a process based on one or another new alternative rather than that primitive antique—the silver of photography's infancy.

An Electrical Image

Xerographic film is coated with a substance that becomes electrically conductive when exposed to light. Before exposure, this "photoconductor" is sprayed with a positive electrical charge. Wherever light strikes, the material conducts charge away through a layer beneath the coating (below). Colored, negatively charged "toner" particles are brushed or washed over the film, and since opposite charges attract, the toner particles are drawn to the positive charges remaining on the film. When heated the particles fuse and form a positive image (right).

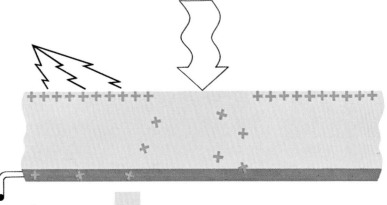

+ Positive charge   Photoconductor

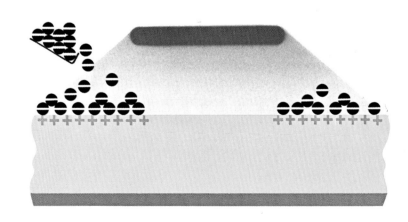

⬒ Negatively charged toner particle

The Darkroom Explosion

At-home processing is bigger than ever, thanks to new color chemistry, paper and enlargers—plus the wonderful chance it presents to control the results

A striking development in photography during 1974 was as old as photography itself. Photographers across the country, caught up in a whirlwind of renewed interest in do-it-yourself processing, were entering the darkroom—many for the first time—to mix chemicals, slip negatives into enlargers, and pull prints from fixer baths. Equipment dealers from Atlanta to Los Angeles used words like "skyrocket" to describe the escalation in their sales.

"Ten years ago the darkroom business was dead. Now it seems to be thriving." That observation by a midwestern photographer was confirmed by dealers in all parts of the country. A Washington, D.C., photography store owner reported that his sales of enlargers, easels, trays, timers, printing papers, and packaged chemicals had increased 50 per cent or more during the year. In Chicago, the manager of a large photography shop was amazed by the volume of high-priced equipment he sold: "They don't care what it costs—they want the best." In some affluent California communities, building a darkroom has acquired the status of owning a sauna or a temperature-controlled wine cellar. In Long Beach, where sales were up a quarter of a million dollars over 1973, a shop owner said: "I've seen people move a kid out of a bedroom to install a darkroom."

Leading the home-processing revival has been an explosion of interest in color printing. "Color is coming to the amateurs," said a northern Delaware shop owner. An Oak Park, Illinois, dealer reported: "I've seen sales of color equipment overtake black-and-white within the past year." Throughout the United States, in fact, the number of home darkrooms equipped to process color doubled. Behind the color boom is a new generation of processing and enlarging equipment. In 1974 four leading manufacturers introduced color enlargers. These enlargers not only simplify printing but also make color equipment available to the amateur for the first time at a reasonable price. bottom-of-the-line models can be purchased for $240. An up-to-date color enlarger (page 105) contains a filtration system in which "dichroic" filters separate a beam of white light into complementary colors to produce a properly modified color beam for exposure. The mixture of colors in the beam can be adjusted at the turn of a dial to give perfect results every time.

Ease of use, low price, and perfect results are not terms that have been with color printing for very long. During the last two decades, a color printer has had to spend 35 minutes, a third of them in complete darkness, to produce a single color print. He inserted dye filters by hand into his enlarger—filters that tended to fade and were easily scratched. He had to maintain a constant temperature of 85° and this required costly equipment. His paper took as long as an hour to dry in the open air. Finally, when he had completed his print, he often found to his dismay that his unreliable acetate filters had produced an image that was grossly distorted in color. Though this lengthy, costly, often unrewarding process was slightly improved over the years, it is easy to see why it found few adherents.

Today, color darkrooms have been virtually revolutionized. Dichroics have replaced the dye filters. Pre-packaged chemicals that can be used at room temperature have reduced the number of baths needed to make a color print from seven in the past to two or three now. The exposed print now goes into an inexpensive, plastic light-tight drum, and printing is completed in ordinary light. New resin-coated paper also aids speed and accuracy. (Because resin-coated paper is plastic laminated, chemicals do not penetrate its fibers and it can be quickly washed and dried.) From start to finish the new color process can take as little as 10 minutes—just about the time needed to make a black-and-white print.

Color darkrooms have turned up in some unlikely places—a notable example is the rectory of the Blessed Sacrament Roman Catholic Church in Boston. Father Arthur J. Colby, a member of the order of Vincentian Fathers, began taking pictures as a young missionary in China in 1946. Now he works in and around Boston, where he was born, photographing neighborhood children and their families. Last summer, when Father Colby decided to set up a simple color darkroom in a storage room of the rectory basement, he bought a compact $350 enlarger with a color head, and installed a used color analyzer. The analyzer allows Father Colby to determine the proper filtration and exposure settings for lifelike flesh tones. Once he has exposed his enlarged print, he carries it from the storage room to an adjacent laundry room for the next steps in the process—developing, fixing, and washing. Even in this primitive setup Father Colby makes as many as 40 color prints a day.

That the lure of color is bringing photographers back into the darkroom is fitting; color pulled many of them out of it some 20 or 25 years ago. A look at some photographic history will show why.

In the early stages there were few manufactured supplies: photographers had to coat paper, metal, or glass with photosensitive emulsions before they could take their pictures, and then they had to process their own negatives and prints. By the late 1880s, photographers could buy pre-coated roll film and take advantage of a system whereby they returned exposed black-and-white film to the manufacturer and received finished prints back in the mail. The dedicated hobbyist, however, continued to work in a home lab, developing his own negatives and making contact prints by exposing them to sunlight (a practical enlarger for amateurs had yet to be perfected). Then, as now, photography was considered an especially appropriate hobby for the young, and in the 1890s successful canvassers for subscriptions to *Youth's Companion* received a bonus: a ''photo outfit'' for their darkrooms, complete with a contact printer and chemicals. For the serious amateur, a magazine called *The Darkroom* flourished during the first decades of the 1900s.

Interest in darkrooms even began to increase sharply in the 1930s, when 35mm cameras became popular. The revolutionary hand-held cameras exposed a compact, small-format film that could easily be developed in a handy, light-tight tank, and enlarging the print from a developed negative gave the photographer enormous freedom to manipulate the final image. He could crop a photograph by printing only part of the negative; he could reduce or increase exposure time to darken or lighten parts of the print; he could adjust the position and tilt of his easel for special effects. Darkrooms multiplied throughout the 1930s and 1940s.

By the mid-1950s, however, color photography had become enormously popular, and for a while that enthusiasm spelled the eclipse of the darkroom. Color-reversal film, which produced transparencies when processed, did not need a home darkroom for the best results; in fact, most color-reversal film had to be sent to a laboratory for processing. Color transparencies—with their intense, jewel-like tones and their ability to project an image to impressive dimensions—seduced serious amateurs from black and white, and many abandoned their darkrooms.

Most of the photographers who switched to color in those days have remained loyal to their collections of small, square-framed transparencies. Perhaps from force of habit, today's long-time photography buff usually takes color slides exclusively, and does not process them; his interest in the technical aspects of photography is generally limited to his camera and its attendant lenses. It is possible, however, that last year's harvest of new color enlargers may lure even these die-hards into the ranks of the darkroom recruits. Meanwhile, the most single-minded darkroom fans come primarily from the most populous age group in the country: the under-30-year-olds. They are compleat photographers, who follow a picture from the first glimpse of an image in the real world through to its magical reappearance in the developing tray.

A substantial number of these darkroom operatives were first introduced to the craft in a formal classroom. Photography courses, common in colleges, are now turning up in high schools and even elementary schools. "Youngsters who never thought of photography are learning about it in school," says a dealer in Buffalo, New York, "and it is leading them to buy their own darkroom equipment." The fact is not surprising; as photographic skills go, darkroom technique is comparatively easy to learn. Students start the semester knowing nothing and end it knowing how to make a print. Such visible and rapid progress is gratifying to educators and students alike—thus, the courses proliferate. Darkroom work is also representative of a general revival of interest in crafts among young people, who are weaving their own fabrics, baking their own bread—and processing their own pictures.

Current developments in camera design are also fueling the darkroom explosion. Many new cameras have electronic circuitry that automatically sets the correct aperture or shutter speed. Chosen because they solve touchy problems at the picture-taking stage, these "thinking" cameras still leave to the home lab many of the critical choices and decisions that photographers delight in. Deliberate darkroom manipulation enjoyed a special vogue in 1974, with students and hobbyists increasingly interested in multiple images, solarization, and high contrast. The results of a 1974 national photography competition for students, exhibited during the summer in New York City, demonstrated that young people had discovered the darkroom was more than a place where negatives get enlarged and printed. Nearly a third of the award winners were high-contrast prints or prints made from two or more negatives —in other words, pictures that were at least partly created in a darkroom, rather than in a camera.

Al Francekevich, a photographer who teaches and writes about darkroom techniques, has noticed that his students often depend on the darkroom to rescue their work from the commonplace. Most of the young photographers Francekevich knows reject the concept of planning a picture ahead of time and setting it up in a studio. They much prefer off-the-cuff, on-the-street, available-light shooting. "To them the discovery of a picture is the creative kick," he says, "not visualizing what they want and then carefully arranging it. Their approach makes the darkroom even more important—it enables them to extend control over the work *after* the exposure in order to make up for the lack of control before exposure. They need the darkroom to alter the way the picture looks—to break the sameness of location shooting."

Educated in darkroom skills with black and white, these young hobbyists can easily make the jump to color—now that simplified, inexpensive color equipment is available to them. Certainly, color printing is fully capable of allowing for the manipulation of tones and the combination of images that appeal to today's student. It seems only a question of time before sophisticated color techniques will be as effectively mastered by these young darkroom magicians as black-and-white techniques are now. For only in a darkroom can a photographer follow his vision to a true conclusion—whether he works in color or in black and white—determining the final darkness of a sky, overseeing the precise play of light and color across a face, concealing here, revealing there. Actually exposing a negative is one medium, processing and printing it another. In 1974, amateur photographers made clear that they want to practice their art on both levels; and with the introduction of so much new darkroom equipment, it became equally clear that the photography industry was well positioned to meet their needs.

Everyman's Color Enlarger

What set off a burst of activity in darkrooms around the world in 1974 was growing interest in the color print, and what lighted the fuse for color was store-counter loads of new equipment—most significantly color enlargers that provided greater versatility, better color quality and easier operation. Four manufacturers—Beseler, Durst, Minolta and Omega—jumped into the market with such enlargers, all of them quite similar in design. Their cost was modest in comparison with that of professional lab equipment—$250 to $650 list—and thousands of the new models were eagerly snapped up in the first few months after their appearance.

The new enlargers followed hard after other recent developments that help simplify color work. Resin-coated color-printing papers and improved formulas for processing chemicals (PHOTOGRAPHY YEAR/1974, pages 190-199) turn out prints much more quickly and easily than their predecessors were able to, reducing a hitherto tedious seven-step job to a two- or three-step routine that can be completed in as little as five minutes.

But the new enlargers themselves offer the greatest simplifications of all by adjusting color balance with the setting of a few knobs. In place of the dye filters that previously had to be assembled and placed in the light beam to control its color, they use built-in precision filters of a type called dichroic.

Each filter can separate a beam of white light into two complementary colors; and working together they modify the color composition of the beam from the enlarger lamp (Dichroic filters are discussed in detail on pages 106-107.)

To help adjust the filters so that they balance color properly, an auxiliary piece of equipment called color negative analyzer eliminates much trial-and-error testing. With the aid of a photosensitive cell, this instrument analyzes the color values of the projected image at a single spot on the enlarger easel or gives an average reading for the whole image when held under the enlarger lens. Its meter then indicates settings for the filter control knobs on the enlarger.

The analyzer must be calibrated for each kind of paper and processing chemical employed; to avoid repeated recalibration, most photographers standardize on one system. The analyzer is calibrated by using it to gauge colors produced when the enlarger filters are known to be properly set for one sample negative (this initial setting must be established by trial and error). From that point on, the analyzer uses its knowledge of the kind of print its owner likes. It will evaluate an unprinted negative, determine the color corrections needed for the enlarger light beam, and indicate the correct exposure—to produce what the owner should consider a print in perfect shades of color.

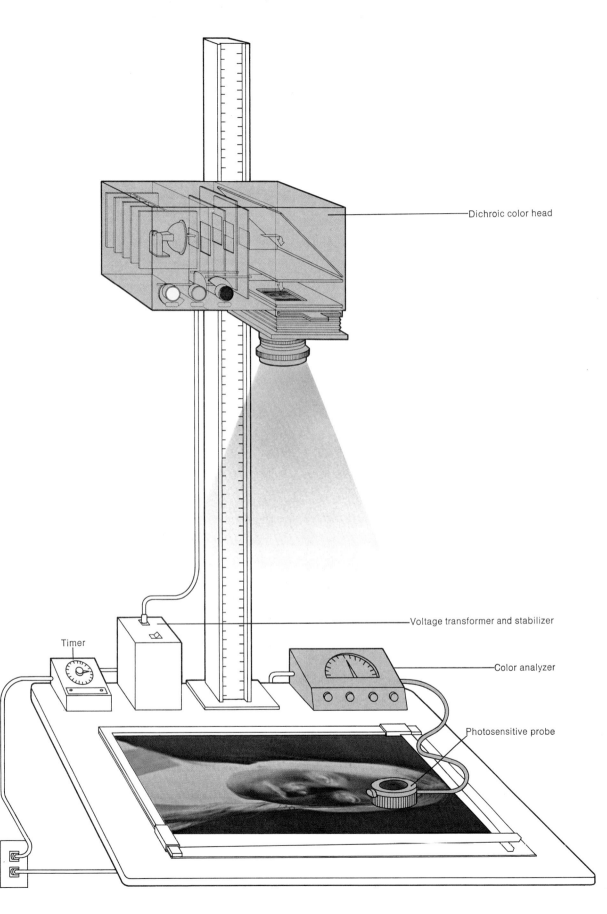

Dichroic color head

Voltage transformer and stabilizer

Timer

Color analyzer

Photosensitive probe

Before printing paper is exposed in a color enlarger, the image projected on the enlarger board is evaluated with the analyzer and its photosensitive probe. Yellow, magenta and cyan color corrections, registered individually on the analyzer meter, are applied to the light beam by turning the three knobs on the color head to position the dichroic filters (pages 106-107). A fourth analyzer reading determines exposure time to be set on the automatic timer. The lamp in the color head is plugged into a combination transformer and voltage stabilizer that adjusts the house voltage and keeps it constant.

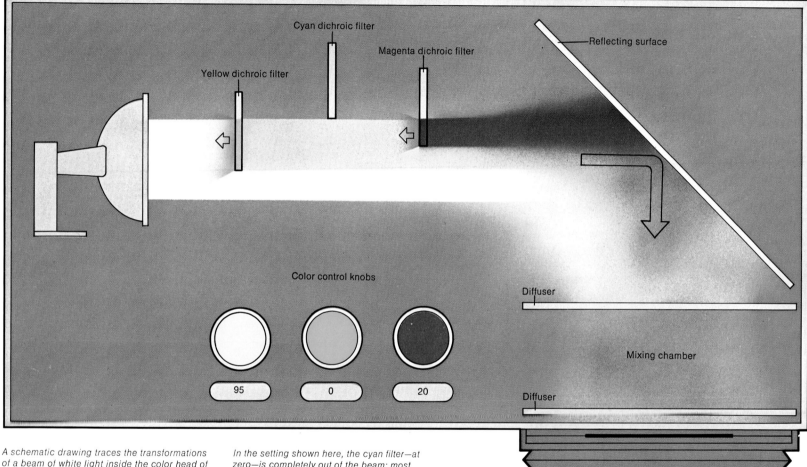

Yellow dichroic filter

Cyan dichroic filter

Magenta dichroic filter

Reflecting surface

Color control knobs

95   0   20

Diffuser

Mixing chamber

Diffuser

A schematic drawing traces the transformations of a beam of white light inside the color head of an enlarger. Three knobs, coded in yellow, cyan and magenta, have been turned to adjust the positions of corresponding dichroic filters in the path of the white light from the enlarger lamp, correcting the color composition of the light to give a pleasing print. Under each knob, a number indicates how much of the beam is intercepted by the filter it controls.

In the setting shown here, the cyan filter—at zero—is completely out of the beam; most negatives do not need cyan correction. Beyond the filters, light is deflected into a mixing chamber, where translucent glass diffusers blend the beam's color components. A thoroughly homogenized beam, from which unwanted colors have been removed in predetermined amounts by the filters, will move through the negative to strike the paper.

A dichroic filter removes an unwanted color from the mixture making up white light by reflecting that color and transmitting the rest. In this photograph of light beams intercepted by dichroic filters, both the reflected and transmitted colors are clearly visible: green light is reflected by the magenta filter, red by the cyan filter and blue by the yellow filter.

The advantage of a dichroic filter is documented in these graphs of the light transmitted by a dye filter (top) and a dichroic filter (bottom). Both are magenta filters, designed to block green light, but the flatter, steep-sided trough of the dichroic's curve indicates a more uniform blocking of all shades of green, and a more uniform transmission of other colors.

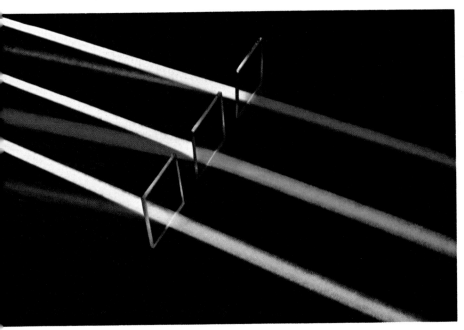

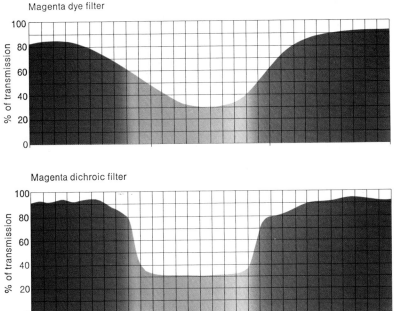

Magenta dye filter

Magenta dichroic filter

Dichroic filters—from spacecraft to home darkrooms

Like freeze-dried foods and palm-sized computers, dichroic filters came to maturity in the course of the space program; later, they were adapted to everyday uses, and since the late 1960s they have been incorporated in photographic equipment. In this short space of time, they have revolutionized color enlarging.

The dichroic filter is a piece of glass coated with extremely thin, transparent layers of nonmetallic compounds. The coatings are deposited by a vacuum process similar to the one used in lens coating *(page 90);* their number and com-

position depend on the colors that the filter is designed to separate.

Like the lens coatings, they work by bouncing specific wavelengths of light—hues of color. Only a part of the light, consisting of a predetermined color, passes through the filter *(above, left).*

Now that dichroic filters can be produced in commercial quantities, they are rapidly supplanting the filters made of dyed gelatin or acetate that have been used. Dichroics last longer than the older types; what is more important, they are more versatile and they perform with far

greater precision. As shown in the graphs above, dichroics block unwanted colors with much greater accuracy. At the same time, they can provide a comprehensive and continuous range of color intensity, blocking more or less light as they are moved into and out of the path of a light beam; in contrast, dye filters can be made in only a limited number of densities, and are not variable. Taken together, the precise filtering and versatile adjustments of the dichroics turn a beam of white light into the color mixture that ensures a perfect print.

Cameras and Equipment

The 110 Bandwagon

When Kodak introduced 110 film in 1972, camera and projector designers around the world hurried to their drawing boards to take advantage of the convenience and compactness offered by the new film. The results finally showed up in 1974 at Photokina, where more than a dozen 110 cameras and several new projectors were put on display by manufacturers from Australia, Japan, and West Germany. Most interesting of them: a tiny Rollei, a fast Canon, a Fujica with a system to help prevent camera-shake blurring, a fast-acting Hanimex slide projector, and a projector from Leitz that gives a brilliant image.

The smallest of all 110s, the Rollei A110, measures 1.3 x 1.8 x 3.4 inches and weighs six and a half ounces. It has a four-element 23mm f/2.8 Tessar lens and offers one-step convenience with a cover that automatically cocks the shutter and advances the film as it opens.

Exposure is automatically controlled, both shutter and diaphragm being set by a silicon cell, which is more sensitive and reacts more quickly than the cadmium sulfide cell commonly used to gauge exposure. Its quick response provides a bonus, giving automatic exposure control when regular flash cubes are used; the meter gauges light reflected back from the subject and regulates the exposure accordingly.

If the Rollei is the smallest 110, the fastest is the Canon 110 ED with a coated, five-element f/2 lens. This camera also includes a feature unusual in 110 cameras: a dial that can be set to record the date or other numerical information, in the lower right-hand corner of the picture frame. The automatic exposure system sets shutter speed, leaving the aperture to be chosen by the photographer. An electronic flash is an accessory, eliminating the need to carry around bulky flash cubes.

The Fujica 600 has a special warning when the automatic exposure system selects a slow speed that might cause problems with camera-shake. When the exposure control sets the shutter speed below 1/30 second, a warning light goes on in the rangefinder—as it does in some other 110 cameras—but as a further precaution the shutter release locks. A lever overrides the lock, so speeds as slow as four seconds can be used.

Among the new 110 slide projectors, the Hanimex Rondette 110 offers fast action. Instead of the usual tray, it has a flexible belt that can hold 120 slides and show them at a rate of more than three per second, enabling the projector to run off a rapid sequence of slides that can simulate motion, time lapse, zoom and animation.

The new Leitz Pradovit Color 110 gives the brightest image of all the 110 projectors; it has a filtering arrangement in its optical system to block heat from its powerful lamp so that slides are not damaged.

The tiny Rollei A110

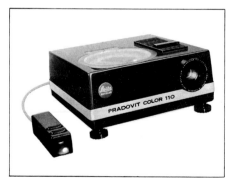

A Leitz Pradovit 110 projector

A Canon 110 ED with flash attachment

Improved 35mm Cameras

Imaginative innovations added new tricks to the automatic 35mm cameras preferred by many amateurs. One camera was made unusually compact; another included the sophisticated dual exposure metering found on few other cameras; and a

A Fujica ST 901 with digital read-out

third adapted a recently developed technique to keep the photographer informed of shutter speed.

The Fujica ST 901, an SLR, is the first camera to display its shutter speed by means of a device that has already made clock watching easier: digital read-out. As its automatic exposure-control system adjusts the shutter, speeds that range from 20 seconds to 1/1000 of a second can be read in bright red numerals at the top of the viewfinder. Because the read-out is electronic, it instantly shows the response of the exposure system to changes in light intensity. Other cameras have used

simpler electronic warnings called LEDs (light-emitting diodes), which are much sturdier than the conventional needle exposure gauge; but until now, no one had made LEDs that formed the numerals of the actual shutter speed.

The numerical shutter speed display provides a special advantage when fast-moving action pictures are taken under a broad range of lighting conditions. If the subject moves into shadows, the automatic exposure system lowers shutter speed, perhaps to a point too slow to stop the action, causing blurred pictures. With the Fujica digital read-out flashing the shutter setting

A twin-metered Vivitar 650/SLX

before each picture is taken, the photographer can readily tell when to open the aperture to compensate for dim light and keep at an action-stopping speed.

Another SLR, the Vivitar 650/ SLX, improves exposure accuracy by allowing the photographer to select either a spot or averaging meter system. Under normal circumstances, the Vivitar makes an average

reading; it can be switched to spot reading when shooting a back-lit subject or a scene with strong contrast between light and dark. The automatic dual exposure system works even when the Vivitar lens is replaced by universal-mount lenses made by other manufacturers.

The long-famous Minox miniature ''spy'' camera now has a 35mm associate—Minox 35 EL. While larger than the spy camera, it is the smallest camera on the market taking standard 35mm film cassettes. Its f/2.8 35mm lens retracts into the camera body so that when closed the unit is almost as compact as a pack of cigarettes. The camera takes full-frame pictures, though, and it is simple to use. When the hinged front of the camera is pulled down, the lens moves forward into position; when the shutter is cocked, the automatic exposure system sets the shutter speed. For focusing, distance must be estimated by the photographer.

A Minox 35 EL

The Rolleiflex SLX. The lens (far right) contains electromagnetic motors to drive aperture and shutter.

Easy-to-Use 2¼ x 2¼ SLRs

Partisans of the 2¼ x 2¼ single-lens reflex found two new cameras on display at Photokina. One, the Kowa Super 66, was notable chiefly for improved interchangeable film backs. The other new model, the Rolleiflex SLX *(above)*, brought almost complete automation to the medium-format camera. It costs about $1,300, but it is filled with electronic gear, including a built-in computer and three electric motors.

Two of the motors are of the type called linear; they do not turn a shaft, like ordinary motors, but operate in a line. And one of them works the shutter—the first completely electric shutter in a camera of this type. The motor moves thin metal leaves between the lens elements to admit or block light; this consistently reliable system eliminates many mechanical parts, re-

ducing the chance of malfunction.

To use the SLX a photographer sets the shutter speed and focuses the lens. Then the camera takes over, on instructions from a computer that spreads electronic circuits over two sides of the body and the front. At lightning speed the computer both gathers information and uses its readings to control aperture, shutter, and film advance.

The film advance is motorized. By setting a switch for sequence shooting and holding the shutter-release button down, the photographer can expose 12 frames in a little over eight seconds—and expose every frame correctly, even if a different aperture setting is required for each exposure. The film advance, however, may be switched off so that multiple exposures on a single frame can be made.

After making an exposure and au-

tomatically advancing the film, the camera turns itself off to save battery power. A light-emitting diode (LED) in the viewing screen flashes a warning when the battery has only enough power for 12 exposures; the entire system shuts down before the battery is completely discharged.

In spite of its sophistication, the SLX is as easy to load as a 110 camera. A plastic cartridge can be preloaded with film; after exposure it drops out when the back of the camera is opened.

The Kowa Super 66 *(below)*, another 2¼ x 2¼ format camera displayed at Photokina, costs about half as much as the Rolleiflex and, what is more unusual, less than the model it supersedes, despite the addition of interchangeable film backs. The L-shaped back has a built-in light shade that drops into place when film is advanced, permitting the photographer to change film in mid-roll without inserting a separate dark slide.

Kowa's Super 66 has interchangeable backs.

New Films

Kodachrome, the first and most popular mass-produced color slide film, is too successful to be tampered with lightly. Only twice has Kodak ventured to change it: in 1962, Kodachrome II, with a speed of ASA 25 replaced the original ASA 10 Kodachrome. In 1963, Kodachrome X with a speed of ASA 64 was added. In 1974, however, Kodak introduced two new Kodachrome films that soon will retire both Kodachrome II and Kodachrome X from the market. This change was only one of several that will affect picture-taking. Other makers of color film also altered

The first new Kodachromes in eleven years

emulsions, and a new Polaroid Land film turns out both negatives and prints more simply.

Kodachrome 25 is only slightly different from the type it replaces, but Kodachrome 64 is considered a major advance. It achieves high speed without dulling colors or introducing extra contrast. By the end of 1975 the old Kodachrome lines may have disappeared from store shelves, but processing for the older films will still be available.

The other new color-slide film is Agfachrome 64. The major change from its predecessor is an increase in speed from ASA 50 to ASA 64.

Among color-print films, Fuji redesigned its high-speed—ASA 100—Fujicolor for a new type labeled F-II. Available in four negative sizes, including the newly popular 110 *(page 108)*, it is said to provide improved chemical stability and better color reproduction. The new film can be processed in Kodak as well as Fuji chemicals.

Polaroid's new black-and-white Type 105 Positive/Negative Land pack film is meant primarily for scientific and other professional purposes, but it may attract more amateur users because it is more convenient than the previous film that also produced both a negative and an instant print. Its predecessor was available only in single sheets for 4 x 5 view cameras or for cameras with specially adapted backs, and it suffered from a quirky characteristic: though it was rated at a speed of ASA 50, it produced the best prints at ASA 64 and the best negatives at ASA 32. To get a good negative, the photographer had to overexpose the print. To get a good positive, he had to underexpose.

The new Type 105 is produced in an eight-sheet pack that fits most standard Polaroid Land cameras as well as the Polaroid backs used with other cameras. And the exposure rating is identical for both print and negative: ASA 75.

The new print and negative sandwich is pulled from the back of a camera just as a familiar Polaroid print is removed. After 45 seconds of developing outside the camera, the print and negative are separated. The print must be coated immediately. The negative emerges with an opaque black coating and must be bathed within three minutes in clear water (or in a sodium sulfite solution, which helps preserve the image). To make this washing step simple, Polaroid produced a portable tank for negative clearing into which the negatives can be dropped as they emerge from the camera.

A negative from Polaroid's Type 105 Land film

An instant print and negative, too

111

Two sizes of Ilfospeed resin-coated paper

The Swing to Resin

The popularity of resin-coated printing papers, first marketed for color use in 1968, was confirmed by new darkroom materials and equipment introduced in 1974. Among them were six new resin-coated papers for black-and-white printing, two dryers, and a specially designed mounting process.

The advantage of resin coating is that it sharply cuts the time required for washing and drying, and manufacturers are now forecasting that within five years nothing but resin-coated stock will be available.

Resin-coated paper has a thin layer of waterproof polyethylene —the resin—on both sides. A light-sensitive emulsion is anchored to the resin coat. Chemicals used in processing never get beyond the resin base, so the print washes clean in two to five minutes rather

than the half hour or more normally required for standard paper. The new paper dries in the open air within 15 minutes. When warm air is circulated around the prints, drying time is cut to less than two minutes.

Ilford has brought out a system for processing resin-coated prints that includes six contrast grades of Ilfospeed paper *(left)*, developer, fixer and a dryer. A print can be processed and dried in four minutes. Kodak is adding new Kodabrome RC paper—available in five contrast grades with smooth glossy or smooth luster surfaces—to its resin-coated line. Unicolor, Inc., is also bringing out resin-coated paper in five contrast grades, available in matte, silk, fine and glossy surfaces. Luminos offers RD-Silk, a warm-toned portrait paper.

Although these resin-coated papers dry in minutes, they cannot be placed on conventional dryers. With a conventional dryer, a print is pressed against a heated metal plate and moisture escapes through the pores of the paper. A resin-coated print cannot be dried in this way because its polyethylene coating does not permit the water to escape. The high temperature used to dry a conventional print can also be damaging, since the resin coat melts at 230° F.

New dryers specially designed for resin-coated papers are beginning to appear. One of the first is the Durst FRC 400 *(right)*, which blows warm air over prints on racks.

Resin-coated papers require new techniques for mounting prints for display because conventional dry-mount tissues do not adhere well to the plastic coating. Turaphot of Germany introduced two types of paper with adhesive backs. One, known in Europe as Thermocoll and in the United States as Luminos RD-ITM, has a heat-sensitive backing. The adhesive coat is made sticky by heating the paper with an iron or mounting press to 150° F.—a temperature low enough to leave the resin coat intact. An alternative approach provided by the same manufacturer is called Tura-Fix Adhesive in Europe and Luminos RD-SST in the United States. After a print is dried, a protective sheet is peeled

The Durst dryer for resin-coated paper

away from the back, exposing an adhesive coating.

In addition to these self-mounting papers, a dry-mounting procedure has been designed specifically for resin-coated papers. The new Seal ColorMount process consists of silicone-treated cover sheets, special tissues, and temperature indicator strips to produce a smooth bonding job on the plastic-coated paper. The indicator strips help guard against under- or overheating.

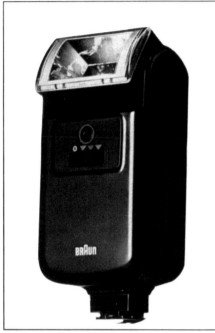

The Braun thyristor electronic flash

Three Energy-Saving Flash Units

An electrical circuit based on the thyristor, a type of transistor, saves battery power in three electronic flash units. The thyristor turns off the power the instant current for the flash is no longer needed.

This new wrinkle works on self-adjusting flashes—those that automatically gauge the amount of light needed for correct exposure. Sensors measure the flash of light bounced back from the subject, and when just the right amount has been reflected for correct exposure—the closer the subject the less light needed—the flash is automatically turned off. Previous models used the same power for all flashes, short or long. When the subject is close to the camera and only a short flash is required, an enormous amount of energy is lost.

The thyristor system prevents this waste by stopping the energy flow at the same time it turns off the flash. Enough energy is saved to shorten the recycling time between exposures and to increase the number of flashes per battery charge.

The effectiveness of the thyristor system is dramatic. When the distance from subject to camera is 20 feet, one of the models, fully charged, can produce 60 flashes before the battery needs to be recharged, and the unit requires eight seconds to recycle. When the subject is only two feet away, the unit is capable of 1,600 flashes, and recycles in just one third of a second. Older automatic flash units get the same number of flashes and require the same recycling time whether the subject is two or 20 feet away.

Essentially similar thyristor systems are offered in three units, costing $150 to $200: the Braun 2000 VarioComputer 40VCR *(left),* the Honeywell Auto/Strobonar 470, and the Metz 218TR Quadrolight.

Brighter Prints from Slides

A simplified version of the Cibachrome process for making color prints from slides, a long-time favorite in European professional laboratories because it gives brilliant color tones, is now available for use in home darkrooms. Most systems create an image by generating dyes in the emulsion during processing; Cibachrome employs paper containing dyes already formed: it is a white plastic sheet coated with a nine-layer emulsion containing three dyes. To make the image, some proportion of each dye is bleached out in the chemical baths.

Prints are produced in the usual way, with an enlarger and processing trays or a drum. But after initial development, a bleach step removes dyes in the emulsion wherever exposed silver grains have been developed. The silver itself is converted to a form that can be dissolved in the fixer. The remaining pattern of lustrous color is the image. The dyes used in the emulsion layers, of the so-called azo type, not only last a long time but also in-

Cibachrome paper, chemicals and processing drum

crease image sharpness; light rays ordinarily scattered by photosensitive particles in the emulsion are absorbed by the dyes before they can blur detail by spreading.

Lenses for Bigger Enlargements

Lenses of shorter focal length designed for standard enlargers—increasing the size of a print by about 70 per cent—were introduced by Schneider at Photokina. The 60mm WA-Componon lens replaces the

Schneider's wide-angle enlarger lens

conventional 80mm enlarger lens for the 2¼ x 2¼ negatives common in twin-lens reflexes; the 80mm lens replaces the 105mm for the 2¼ x 3¼ negatives used in some press cameras.

Using the new lenses, a darkroom worker will get bigger prints or bigger enlargements of details directly on the easel, without having to position his enlarger to project an image on wall or floor. If his standard lens gives 10x magnification with the enlarger head raised to its maximum distance from the easel, the wide-angle lens will make the magnification 13x at the same enlarger setting.

Double-jointed Tripod

On most tripods the legs adjust to different lengths, but all three legs open together to one angle. A new improvement is independently positioned legs: each can be set at any of three different angles for greater flexibility in setting up close shots.

To illustrate the versatility of the smallest and lightest of the new models, for 35mm cameras *(below)*, two legs have been extended while the third is left short and pitched at a sharper angle. The photographer can now take a picture looking straight down; if he tried the same overhead shot with a conventional tripod, the legs might show in the photograph or the tripod could be dangerously unstable.

When the legs are telescoped to their shortest position and spread out to their widest angle, the Gitzo Performance tripods can be set as low as five inches off the ground. The compact model stretches as high as 66 inches; other models go as high as 92 inches.

The versatile Gitzo Sport Performance tripod

A Processing Drum for Film

Unicolor's Film Drum is a plastic cylinder that lies on its side and is rolled back and forth by a motor. A movable piston at one end adjusts the drum for the number and size of film reels. Because the drum rotates the film through a pool of chemicals, the pool need not fill the cylinder; it thus requires lesser amounts of chemicals than conventional tanks, in which the film must be completely submerged.

A Drum for Color Prints

One of the more ingenious gadgets for home color-processing is a hand-cranked drum for developing prints. The device provides even agitation of chemicals and paper for streak-free images—generally attainable only with the use of more costly, motor-driven devices—because the crank moves the drum

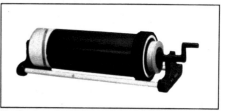

The hand-cranked Paterson Color Print Processor

in two directions simultaneously. As the container rotates, it also slides horizontally back and forth: on each turn a tab on the cradle engages an eccentric groove on the drum to shift it. The British-made Paterson Color Print Processor is available in two sizes, for 8 x 10 and 11 x 14 prints.

Discoveries / 4

Discoveries /4

LUIGI GHIRRI

SHIN SUGINO

ANDERS PETERSEN

DENNIS HEARNE

FRANCO FONTANA

Discoveries

The Quest for New Talent

Out of a field of 26 gifted but unknown photographers, selected from all over the world by a panel of experts, the Editors of Photography Year pick five who seem slated for future renown

Every year the Editors of PHOTOGRAPHY YEAR undertake a search for new and promising photographic talent. The aim of the search is to bring to a wide public the work of serious photographers who are not yet known outside a small circle of local colleagues, critics or teachers. In 1974 the search was conducted on an international scale, with the aid of photographic authorities in Canada, southeast Asia, Europe, and the United States.

The six experts were: Lanfranco Colombo of Milan, whose magazine and gallery are potent forces in Italian photography; Brian Brake, a New Zealand-born freelance photojournalist based in Hong Kong; Helen Johnston, whose San Francisco photography gallery is one of the oldest in America; Sven Andersson, managing director of the most important photographic agency in Scandinavia; Nathan Lyons, photographer, editor and teacher in Rochester, New York; and Lorraine Monk, editor and head of still photography at the National Film Board of Canada, in Ottawa.

Each of these consultants nominated a group of gifted photographers, chosen from scores of possibilities in his respective locality. Under the ground rules, nominations were not to include professional photographers or those who had already achieved substantial recognition through books and magazines, large museum and gallery exhibitions, or through representation in museum collections. But these were the only restrictions placed upon the consultants. Age, sex, and background of the photographers were irrelevant, and all styles, techniques and subjects were eligible. The works of 26 candidates from three continents were submitted by the consultants. The Editors of PHOTOGRAPHY YEAR selected the five finalists whose work appears on the following pages. All have produced work of such high quality that they seem assured of wider recognition in the future. In fact, soon after his work was chosen for this book, one of the five finalists—Franco Fontana—received the honor of an exhibition at the 1974 Photokina in Cologne, Germany.

Fontana, who lives in Italy, is a 41-year-old furniture dealer whose color photographs of seashores, highways and rolling fields verge on the abstract. Shin Sugino, a 28-year-old Japanese-born Canadian, teaches at York University, in Toronto, and edits a photography magazine. His black-and-white records of a voyage of pilgrimage to Europe have the spare simplicity and evocative mystery of traditional Japanese art. Anders Petersen of Sweden, 30 years old, documentarian and photojournalist, strikes a pessimistic note in his photographic study of lonely city dwellers. Another Italian, Luigi Ghirri, age 31, photographs an urban landscape in which cardboard cutouts and advertising posters take the place of people. Dennis Hearne, a 27-year-old American of Irish descent who teaches at the San Francisco Art Institute, presents the countryside and people of rural Ireland in somber black and white—but with a warm feeling for a special way of life.

THE PHOTOGRAPHY YEAR
Panel of Consultants

Top row, left to right

LANFRANCO COLOMBO
Editor of *Fotografia Italiana* and Director of Il
Diaframma photography gallery, Milan

BRIAN BRAKE
Photojournalist and documentary film producer,
Hong Kong

Middle row, left to right

HELEN JOHNSTON
Director of Focus Gallery, San Francisco

SVEN ANDERSSON
Managing Director of Tiofoto Agency, Stockholm

Bottom row, left to right

NATHAN LYONS
Photographer and Director of the Visual Studies
Workshop, Rochester, New York

LORRAINE MONK
Editor and Executive Producer, Still Photography
Division, National Film Board of Canada, Ottawa

Photographers nominated by the Consultants

DINSHAW BALSARA, Hong Kong
HENRI S. COUSINEAU, Moncton, New Brunswick
RALPH H. FERTIG, Galeta, California
*FRANCO FONTANA, Modena, Italy
HANS GEDDA, Stockholm
*LUIGI GHIRRI, Modena, Italy
KENNETH GRAVES, San Francisco
BENNO GROSS, Hong Kong
WERNER HAHN, Hong Kong
*DENNIS HEARNE, San Francisco
JEAN HERMANSSON, Stockholm
EARL KOWALL, Montreal
RICHARD LINK, Buffalo, New York
JOAN LYONS, Rochester, New York
ROGER MERTIN, Rochester, New York
ANNE NOGGLE, Albuquerque, New Mexico
NILS JOHAN NORENLIND, Sollentuna, Sweden
MITCHELL PAYNE, San Francisco
*ANDERS PETERSEN, Stockholm
GIUSEPPE G. PINO, Milan
ERIC RENNER, Alfred, New York
*SHIN SUGINO, Toronto
GEORGE TATGE, Rome
MAURO VALLINOTTO, Milan
TURE WESTBERG, Stockholm
PETER YUNG, Hong Kong

*Work of this photographer is shown on the
following pages.*

Franco Fontana Transmuted Reality

In Italy, a furniture dealer photographs seashores, highways and rolling fields as opulent horizontal designs, suppressing details to create pictures in which shapes and color become the subject matter

The landscapes of Franco Fontana, one of two Italian discoveries, come close to being pure abstractions. Identifiable details dissolve into large areas of clear, muted color organized in broad horizontal stripes that swell and shrink across fields of glowing light. A second look reveals sand dunes, highway stripes, waves, the horizon. To some observers Fontana's banded colors are reminiscent of some of the most advanced types of modern abstract painting, yet his pictures are shot directly from nature, without special filters, and printed straight and full-frame by a commercial laboratory, without any darkroom manipulation. Sometimes Fontana uses an extreme wide-angle lens to broaden the planes, sometimes a telephoto to flatten them. But the abstract look is essentially due to his point of view and his careful choice of location, time of day, and weather.

In choosing a subject, Fontana's preference is for seashores, highways, and rolling fields—places where horizontal layers of varied color dominate the landscape. The five pictures shown here were taken from mid to late afternoon, in calm and unchanging weather. ("I would never shoot a stormy sea," Fontana says, "because its character would obliterate all other meanings.") Most of the pictures were shot with the sun low and behind the photographer, so that its rays flattened out irregularities or salient elements in the landscape.

The results of these procedures are pictures in which the real subjects are not the sea or the rolling fields at which Fontana aimed his camera, but an essence of color and form that the photographer has distilled from those commonplace materials.

Fontana is very clear in his own mind about what he is doing, but this clarity of intention was slow in coming. When he began to photograph he was both conventional and indiscriminate, aiming his camera at everything he saw around him: sunsets, reflections, beautiful things that anybody could see for himself. "Consequently," he says, "I was a reproducer of images, not a discoverer; behind the machine, there was as yet no person. Now I am trying to re-invent the things I see around me, give them shape in my own way. My work is not pure abstraction. It is always based on nature, and in some of my pictures there are miles of space."

Fontana is not a professional photographer. A member of "Dimensione," a small group of dedicated amateurs around Lanfranco Colombo, director of Il Diaframma gallery in Milan, he is part owner and director of a furniture store in Modena that specializes in contemporary Italian design, so, he says, "my working life is still connected with form and color." Now 41, he has been photographing for 12 years, and in the past few years he has begun to be published in Italian art and photography magazines and to be exhibited in small galleries in Italy and elsewhere in Europe.

Taken in Southern Italy, this beach scene
is both a handsome abstract design and a
powerful visual statement about the
Mediterranean Sea. The rich blue wind-rippled
water shades off into green as it nears a sandy
shore, and the ragged shadow at the bottom
completes the composition.

Sky, highway, center stripe and a guardrail on the Brussels-Paris road blend into a muted arrangement of steel gray, reddish brown, green and shades of blue. Taken from a fast-moving car, the picture smoothes out such details as guardrail rivets and roadside stones.

Pastel postcard colors in this view
of an Adriatic beach offset the bare simplicity
of the composition and the bright,
stark row of cabins marching in from the left.
In the foreground, the soft light
of a late afternoon sun casts a subtle blue
shadow across the sand.

Grassy, rolling hills in Puglia, faintly rutted with cart tracks (left), seemed joyous and expressive to the photographer. As he put it, the smoky blue shadows, warmed by highlights of yellow and dark green, "conjured up something 'molto dolce,' very gentle and sweet."

In Romagna, a quiet sea breaks gently on a sandy beach scored by two long, narrow tidal pools that reflect the gray-pink sky. Parallel textures and tints of sky, sea, and sand divide the scene into flat horizontal sections so that the reality of the seashore is almost lost.

Shin Sugino: A Pilgrim's Progress

The simple yet enigmatic pictures of a young Japanese-Canadian photographer record the outcome of a highly personal encounter between East and West

The subjects of Shin Sugino's terse, understated pictures—a round stone, dog tied to a wall, a girl leaping into the sea—could be found, and over looked, by almost anyone. Sugino did not overlook them, and in his picture they are endowed with a supernatural presence. Though apparently common place, Sugino's subjects glow with an inner light. They stand out as if spotl against a dense, dark background that focuses dramatic attention on ther while suggesting a larger and more various world beyond.

The total effect is mysterious and complex. Yet Sugino's photographs ar esthetically and technically uncomplicated. "I believe image-making alway has to be talking simply," he says. "The simpler the image the stronger th message. Just like Japanese painting."

Traditional Japanese painting often reduces a single subject—a bambo branch, a spray of chrysanthemums—to its simplest possible form in order t bring out its essential characteristics. Sugino does something similar em ploying purely photographic means. He uses a wide-angle lens to create feeling of space, but avoids the lens's distorting effect by working at a con siderable distance from his subjects. To get strong darks and lights he usuall uses a red filter, then overexposes his negative and prints it on high-contras paper, burning and dodging to further intensify contrast.

These are all techniques for black-and-white pictures, and Sugino work mostly in black and white. When he does work in color, which he has recentl begun to do, he keeps it as monochromatic as he can—as close as possible in fact, to the starkness of his black-and-white prints.

The ultimate simplicity of the finished prints is not an end in itself. It is means of expressing Sugino's highly personal relationship to Western civi lization. Though he was born in Japan and grew up there, he was educated in a Catholic orphanage by European and American nuns and priests. At 19, he emigrated to Canada as an apprentice printer, and he later became Canadian citizen.

Torn between two worlds, the Eastern world of his Japanese ancestry and childhood and the Western world of his education and adult life, Sugino wen to Europe in 1973 on what he describes as a kind of pilgrimage, to see for him self the sources of Western culture. He traveled through Spain, Portugal, Swit zerland and France, looking at everything with passionate curiosity. As turned out, the sights that impressed him most were not the much photo graphed grand monuments of art, architecture and history, but little everyda things—which in his pictures acquire the otherworldly authority of a sunli gargoyle suddenly stumbled upon in the dimness of a great cathedral.

All the photographs on the following pages were taken on Sugino's 197 trip to Europe. They are part of a sequence called Pilgrimage, which wa shown in 1974 at The National Film Board gallery in Ottawa.

On the lawn of a hotel in Interlaken, Switzerland, three garden chairs drawn up around a small covered table are as fussily adorned and decorous as the ladies who will soon sit down to tea. The photographer used a red filter to heighten the contrast between grass and chairs.

Down a dark evening street in Marseilles, a blind man walks with a confident air. The street is empty and the windows opening onto it are shuttered, but the walker remains unaware of the strangely ominous atmosphere.

On the Spanish tourist island of Ibiza, the
photographer found this small dog tied to a nail
in a wall. Like a guardian of secrets, the dog
is alert—but also a bit curious, and not
quite decided whether to snarl or wag his tail.

The round stone sitting in a pool of light is one
of 1,400 placed along a road in a Barcelona park
designed by the early 20th Century Spanish
architect Antonio Gaudí. In Sugino's photograph
the stone becomes a mysterious moon rising from
a terrestrial Milky Way.

*A young girl seems to leap into the clouds—
though she is merely jumping off a jetty in
the Portuguese resort of Cascais. The inexplicably
darkened sky and water at the left transform
an otherwise ordinary shot into the pictorial
equivalent of a leap into the dark.*

Anders Petersen: Amusement Park

A Swede who spent two years photographing pleasure-seekers makes a gloomy comment on loneliness, and on the faltering attempts of ordinary people to escape it

In his pictures of life at an amusement park, Anders Petersen depicts a wor in which lonely people seek pleasure without ever finding it. Middle-aged cou ples with every bulge, wrinkle, and blemish clearly showing move slow around a dance floor. Teenagers wait for admittance to a pub with the stol docility of cattle being led to the slaughter. The happiest people are stunte clowns and jokers who mug for the camera, resigned to the cramped emp ness of their lives.

Petersen photographs real people in real locations. His subjects a generally drawn from the lower ranks of the working classes—shop girls, ra way clerks, sailors, prostitutes, or the unemployed. His settings are publ places—streets, parks, dance halls, bars. To achieve the greatest realis possible, he eschews complicated equipment and studio lighting. Using on one small 35mm single-lens reflex camera loaded with high-speed film, he sta tions himself at a spot where a neon sign or other available light source w give him the necessary illumination. He waits there, quietly, until he feels th his presence is no longer disturbing to the people around him; then h begins to shoot.

The resulting pictures have the appearance of candid photographs eve though, in fact, many of them are posed. The style is stark, brutal, even ugl Like many young photographers, 30-year-old Petersen is more interested i the social and political uses of photography than in the fine points of prin making and technique. "I don't want to hang photographs on a wall as a sta tus thing," he says. "I want my photography to serve as means o communication between people. There are so many lonely people in th world. If they can see photographs of others like themselves they will ur derstand they are not so different not so alone."

Petersen tries to approach the people he photographs as a member o their group, not as an outsider. "You must be with them first as a huma being, and second as a photographer," he says. To take the pictures on th following pages he spent two years at the dance halls, pavilions and pubs o Gröna Lund amusement park in central Stockholm. He has also photographe the sailors and prostitutes of Hamburg's notorious Reeperbahn red-light dis trict—a series that has been widely shown and praised in Europe—and h was commissioned by the Swedish government to document the lives of im migrant workers, predominantly Mediterranean, who are playing an importal part in Sweden's economic life.

In all of these projects what Petersen has achieved is not so much ob jective reportage as a pessimistic vision of modern urban life, in which colo isolated people come together in a vain search for human contact an warmth. The vision may be personal and subjective, but there is enough trut in it to strike home to everyone.

On a Sunday night at the dance pavilion of
the Gröna Lund amusement park in Stockholm,
couples dance under a canopy lined with light
bulbs. Neither young nor old, neither handsome
nor ugly, the dancers are typical of the park's
more than 1,400,000 annual visitors.

At the door of Mollbergs, a busy pub at Gröna Lund, a short, grimacing doorkeeper bars the way to a group of young people waiting outside. The doorkeeper is not an employee but a habitué of the pub who enjoys the sense of importance he gets from his self-appointed task.

Two regulars at Mollbergs pub pose for a double portrait. The man on the left is known to the pub's patrons for having a brother in the Royal Opera Company of Stockholm. His friend with the hat and the hot dog carries on a nightly flirtation with the pub's 73-year-old pianist, Lily.

A pretty girl and the young man she has met that evening embrace under a dart board in a pub just outside the amusement park. They have been playing darts and talking, and now must decide whether they will part or go off together; this pub—the last to close—is the final stopping place for visitors to the park.

This young man, whom the photographer knows
only by his first name, Rickard, often wanders
through the amusement park "looking around,
seeking someone." Shy and sensitive, he
dreams of becoming a photographer.
To Petersen he is typical of the lost people
searching for companionship in the park.

Luigi Ghirri: Cardboard Cityscapes

A young Italian photographs a strange world of substitutes and imitations in which advertising posters and painted rainbows overwhelm the real people and objects they represent

In Italian photographer's Luigi Ghirri's view of life, man-made images, ranging from cardboard cutouts and advertisements to statuary, have taken the places of real people, objects, and feelings. A cardboard camel seems to walk across a road. In a florist's window display, living flowers blend with photographed flowers. A rainbow is seen not in the sky but painted on the side of a building. The pretty girl outside a camera store is actually a life-sized photograph that has been cut out and mounted on cardboard. The dramatic images that fill a Renaissance sculpture seem to project greater religious emotion than the figures of first communion celebrants who are posed woodenly before it.

In Europe, as in America, such surrealistic juxtapositions are common, but most people do not notice them. Ghirri finds both the juxtapositions and their ready acceptance very strange. "The modern world," he comments, "unthinkingly contents itself with surrogates, with printed cardboard versions of meadows, with painted rainbows—and sometimes it accepts these more easily than real things."

In his photographs Ghirri brings out this view in subtle yet powerful ways—setting his subjects among other fantastic creations and against the background of city streets and squares. "I turned to photography," he says "because it seemed the medium most suited to the epoch we are in. It is very precise and makes it possible to document and reveal aspects of reality." He uses no special tricks to capture that reality, photographing what he sees, and having his work developed and printed full-frame in a commercial laboratory Ghirri admires a number of American documentary photographers—particularly Walker Evans, Paul Strand and Lee Friedlander—and strives for the same "clear and limpid views of reality, the same cold and impartial vision" that he finds in the work of these men.

Though he travels and photographs in Holland and Switzerland as well as in his native Italy, Ghirri is most inspired by what he sees as he drives from his apartment to his job as a draftsman in a big office building in central Modena: urban sprawl, green spaces within the city, citified suburbs. "This is the life I have to live every day," he says, "and the one I can therefore best propose as a new landscape for close and detailed analysis. The images find here, isolated from their habitual surroundings, can be stated photographically in a different context."

Like the other Italian discovery, Franco Fontana, who lives in the same apartment building in Modena, Luigi Ghirri is a member of the Dimensione group of serious amateurs founded by Lanfranco Colombo, director of Il Diaframma gallery in Milan. At the age of 30, Ghirri has just embarked on the round of exhibitions and publications that is the beginning of recognition for photographers. This is his first appearance in an American publication.

A giant pair of legs with a sunburst for
a body dominates the plaza of a small Italian city.
An advertisement for an Italian circus on ice, the
truncated giantess appears as solid and three-
dimensional as the houses and trucks behind her.

A cartoon camel made of cardboard and wood grins from a Swiss highway. Though Ghirri's photograph establishes the camel and its two-foot-high cigarette box as a conspicuous feature of the road, the motorists hurtling by will scarcely glimpse the figure.

At first glance she appears real—but the smiling girl with the camera slung around her neck is actually a two-dimensional cutout advertisement in the dark hallway of a provincial photography shop. The giveaway is the triangle of light-gray cardboard between her arm and her halter.

In a parody of a conventional first communion picture, two solemn little girls in new white dresses stand as stiff and rigid as dolls; behind them, stone figures bend and twist in lifelike agony in a Renaissance Pietà—a sculpture of Christ mourned by his mother.

An 18th Century horseman rides along a hilltop
overlooking a 20th Century beach resort.
Both are display pieces in a shop window, the
cardboard horseman advertising chocolate,
the beach a photograph from a travel poster.

On the side of a paint factory a series of rainbow
stripes creates a more solid and startling
impression than a real rainbow would. To the
photographer, such substitutions of artfully
designed copies for reality permeate urban life.

In a florist's show window fact and fiction are inextricably intertwined. Photographed as part of a portrait in the window, the flowers held by the little girl seem to extend out of her picture to blend with the real flowers on display.

Dennis Hearne: The Ould Sod Revisited

An American descendant of Irish immigrants depicts the land of his ancestors with affection and respect

Dennis Hearne's black-and-white photographs of rural Ireland capture a world in which rocky fields rimmed by old stone walls slope down to the sea, a prized pig is loved like a pet, stone cottages still have thatched roofs, and a braided horse's mane or a cinched-up haystack can become a work of folk art. In this world life is still close to the earth, and the endlessly repeated cycle of the seasons imposes unalterable patterns on people and places.

"In cities the scene is always changing," Hearne explains, "and in photographs of urban life you get inexplicable and bizarre images. But in Ireland this is not so. There things are built to last, and though you are always in the present you are always looking at the past. There is a certain silence and a tendency for things to repeat themselves. My aim is to try to realize the silence and the cycles of the country."

Hearne's Ireland is far from the bloody violence of Belfast made familiar by photojournalists. Up to a point it is a quaint and picturesque world in which life looks much the same as it did a century ago. But Hearne's pictures have a dark and gritty look, and his probing camera is in search of deeper things than local color or antiquarian charm. His Ireland is a real place where real people live, work, and play. It is a poor, even a hard place, though it has a rugged, honest sort of beauty. Hearne catches its people off guard, in moments of leisure and moments of affection, and despite the sometimes forbidding look of their land, it is clear from Hearne's pictures that they love the place.

The underlying motive behind Hearne's pictures is his own deep interest in Ireland and the Irish. Though he was born in New Hampshire and now lives in California, where he holds a post in the Photography Department of the San Francisco Art Institute, Hearne is himself of Irish ancestry; a great-uncle still lives in County Kilkenny, in the southeastern part of the country. Hearne photographed Ireland to better his own understanding of his Irish heritage. But his pictures of Ireland are only a part of a larger project. Eventually they will form the opening of a three-part series that will, in its entirety, constitute a photographic account of the Hearnes's long westward migration, from Ireland to New England, then on to California. The photographer calls this first part of the series "Foreign Correspondence. Ir." ("Ir" is not only an abbreviation of "Ireland," but also the name of a mythological father of the Irish people and of the country itself.)

To assemble these photographs Hearne visited Ireland in 1972 and 1973, traveling throughout the Republic with little more than two small cameras and a change of clothes—talking to people, looking, shooting. A third trip, aided by a grant from the National Endowment for the Arts, is planned for 1975. The result of this long search is already clear: a series of strong pictures in which the simplicities Hearne discovers in rural Ireland are inferentially contrasted with the anxieties he recognizes in urban America.

On his farm in County Kilkenny, Pater Sean,
the photographer's great-uncle, rubs and pets a
favorite white sow, who suffers the display
of affection with sleepy indifference. The
picture was made in Sean's "haggard," or hay
yard, an open area between house and barn.

Discoveries/**Dennis Hearne**

*Afternoon sun strikes the coast of County
Galway, where treeless, rocky fields separated
by meandering stone walls line the shore.
The crumbling remains of a long-abandoned
farmhouse on the hill are a grim reminder
of the Great Famine of the 1840s, which hit this
part of Ireland worst of all.*

ramed by the small round window at the
nd of their car, an Irish brother and sister
t out a long train ride through the
ountryside south of Dublin. They stare out
to space, bored, listless and indifferent.

A haystack stands in a field in County Donegal, resembling one of the stone burial mounds built by Ireland's earliest inhabitants. Tying hay with a spiraling "sugan," or hay rope, is a traditional practice, echoing an almost obsessive use of the spiral in early Irish art.

At Puck Faire, a famous midsummer fair in County Kerry, the photographer made this close-up of a horse's braided mane against some nearby buildings. The picture is almost abstract, but it suggests the intimate relationship between man and nature that still exists in rural Ireland.

151

This farmer's cottage is typical of the picturesque, primitive architecture found on the Aran Islands, off the coast of County Galway. Stone walls, often windowless, are coated with whitewashed plaster, and the thatched roof is secured against wind and rain by ropes tied to pegs in the end walls.

At the bar of a pub in Kinsale, County Cork,
two patrons take an afternoon break from a long
day's work. The postman, in the foreground,
rests his head on his hand, while his friend rubs
his eyes between puffs on his pipe. Although
candid in feeling, the photograph was actually
made at the pipe smoker's request.

153

In rural County Cork a mule swishes its tail and gazes over scrub-covered fields. Telephone poles visible over the top of a small rise (right) herald the arrival of industrial civilization, but in every other respect this pastoral scene could be lifted from the 18th Century.

Trends / 5

The Thirties Style   158

The Thirties Style/ EDWARD STEICHEN: *Countess Edith di Zoppola in Schiaparelli pajamas,* 1931

Rediscovering a Lost Era: The Thirties Style

The high-style fashion and advertising photographs of four decades ago—never taken very seriously in their own time—are enjoying a respectful revival in the 1970s

by Gene Thornton

Most Americans think of the Thirties Style of photography in terms of social documentation and photojournalism: grim studies of poverty-stricken, dust-bowl families by the photographers of the Farm Security Administration, or horrifying views of famine and war by the early photo-reporters of LIFE and *Look*. A case might also be made for thinking of Thirties photography in terms of the rocks and plant forms recorded in pin-sharp focus by the California-based photographers who called themselves the f/64 Group. But whoever thinks of the Thirties Style in photography as the suave and sophisticated high-style fashion, portrait and advertising photography that appeared in *Vogue* and *Harper's Bazaar,* the leading fashion magazines of the '30s and *Vogue*'s sister publication, dedicated to society and the arts, *Vanity Fair*?

Until recently, these ephemeral works by such photographers as Horst George Hoyningen-Huene and Nickolas Muray have languished largely unseen, half forgotten in the bound volumes of the glossy magazines where they first appeared. Even the advertising and fashion photography of a well-known master like Edward Steichen *(page 157)* has been quietly neglected in favor of his landscapes and portraits.

Now, however, the high style of '30s fashion and advertising photography is being rediscovered—and is winning new appreciation. The revival began in 1970 with an exhibition at the Los Angeles County Museum of Art of the photographs of Hoyningen-Huene. It continued in 1974 at the International Museum of Photography in Rochester, New York, with a 181-image exhibition of the life work of Nickolas Muray, who was a pioneer in color photography for reproduction. Then at the Sonnabend Gallery in New York a show of '30s portraits and fashion photographs by Horst was followed by an exhibition in which Horst's photographs were brought together with those of Hoyningen-Huene and Cecil Beaton, the British stage-designer and portraitist, who also contributed to *Vogue* in the 1930s.

This renewed interest in the high-style photography of the '30s extends to all the arts of the time that share a sophisticated elegance. The movies of Ginger Rogers and Fred Astaire, the sardonic novels of Evelyn Waugh, and the urbane wit of Cole Porter's songs are all enjoying new popularity, along with the stylish opulence of 1930s haute couture, prominently featured in a 1974 exhibition at The Costume Institute of New York's Metropolitan Museum of Art. Perhaps most significant, a five-day exhibition at New York's Radio City Music Hall helped focus new attention on the '30s fashion in architecture and interior decoration—the Art Deco Style.

Art Deco, launched in Paris in 1925 at the Exposition Internationale des Arts Décoratifs, combined the sharp outlines and simplified forms of modern painting with the primitive yet sophisticated vigor of Aztec architecture. It

Mrs. Tudor Wilkinson, an English model and
Ziegfeld Follies star who married a wealthy
American sportsman and art patron, sits on top
of a classical column. The plain background
panels of black and gray provide the perfect foil
for her cool beauty, contributing to the elegant
simplicity of this typical example of the
Thirties Style of fashion-magazine photography.

GEORGE HOYNÍNGEN-HUENE: *Mrs. Tudor Wilkinson*, 1931

spread throughout America in the '30s, producing such monuments as the Chrysler Building in New York, and encouraging photographers like Margaret Bourke-White—best known in the early '30s for her pictures of architecture and industry—to emphasize the beauties of abstract design.

The result of this revival has been a new view of the '30s. This troubled and distressing era is now seen, thanks largely to the Thirties Style photographers, to have had a bright and glittering, if artificial, surface. In the world of the Great Depression and the rise of totalitarianism, people were suffering and dying, but there was another world, calm and luxurious, in which beautiful ladies in expensive gowns descended sweeping staircases or danced on the decks of ocean liners. Partly this second world really did exist, but partly it was the creation of Hollywood movie makers and fashion magazine photographers, whose elegantly unreal creations reflected the hopes and dreams of their enormous audiences.

In photography the inventor and first great master of the high style of the '30s was Edward Steichen. When Steichen started out in the early decades of the century, he, like other serious photographers of the time, followed the prevailing "Pictorialist" style. Hazy and impressionistic, it deliberately imitated paintings or etchings and was not meant for reproduction; the Pictorialists concentrated on handmade prints for display in salon exhibitions. However, in the 1920s, the increased use of photography by high-quality magazines like *Vogue* and *Harper's Bazaar* opened Steichen's eyes to the virtues of making pictures for reproduction. Condé Nast, the publisher of *Vogue,* was eager to employ the very best photographers. He was willing to pay them well, a happy circumstance that enabled them to earn a decent living from photography and achieve a prosperity few salon photographers could hope for. Nast was also able to place pictures before a far larger public than could be reached through salon exhibitions or the art-photography magazines. *Vogue's* circulation was 123,000 compared to the 1,000 circulation of the noted photographic journal, *Camera Work.*

Such tempting possibilities made Steichen decide, he later recalled, "on another apprenticeship. I would learn how to make photographs that would go on the printed page, for now I was determined to reach a large audience." He wished, however, to reach this audience with the latest in photography. As a painter in Paris before the First World War he had become familiar with the revolutionary changes being wrought by artists such as Matisse and Picasso. Parallel changes were taking place in photography, and while Steichen was learning to photograph for the printed page he was also transforming himself from an old-fashioned Pictorialist to what was known in the '20s and the '30s as a Modern Photographer.

Gene Thornton, the author of this article, is a photography critic for *The New York Times* and a contributing editor of *Art News,* as well as a frequent lecturer on art and photography. He recently organized an exhibition of fashion photography.

The difference between a Modern Photographer and an old-fashioned Pictorialist, explained Dr. M. F. Agha, the witty and innovative art director of *Vogue* in the 1930s, was partly a difference between sharp focus and soft focus. The Modern Photographer favored sharp focus, the old-fashioned Pictorialist soft focus. But there was also a significant difference in subject matter, which Agha defined as the difference between Whistler's mother and a yawning hippopotamus. The Pictorialist only photographed interesting and appealing subjects, like Whistler's mother, Agha said, but a Modern Photographer would photograph almost anything provided it was boring, like a vegetable or a rock, or positively revolting, like a yawning hippopotamus. The Pictorialist would photograph Whistler's mother in a soft-edged, atmospheric style, suppressing detail in favor of the general effect, but the Modern Photographer insisted on every little detail, photographing his dew-spangled cabbage or his hippopotamus tonsils in a hard-edged, sharp focus that in time came to be thought of as the only true photographic style. The egg was an especially popular subject with Modern Photographers because it enabled them to put the emphasis on form and pattern. The egg was so well thought of, said Agha, that a Modern Photographer who did photograph an appealing subject like a nude would "twist the model so as to make her really look like one or several eggs."

Steichen did not photograph eggs, but he did photograph flower pots and pears, and in the course of his second apprenticeship he spent a whole summer photographing a single teacup and saucer. Then in 1923 he went to New York and got the job of chief photographer for the Condé Nast magazines. His principal assignment while working for Condé Nast was to photograph celebrities for *Vanity Fair,* but he also agreed to take fashion photographs for *Vogue,* and in both areas he introduced the principles of Modern Photography, or as many of them as could be accommodated in the elegant fantasy world of the fashion magazine.

Basic formulas of fashion photography had already been established by Gayne de Meyer, a German baron who was Steichen's principal predecessor at *Vogue.* Baron de Meyer, like Steichen, had started out as a salon Pictorialist. When he came to *Vogue* in 1913 he merely adapted to the needs of fashion illustration the typical pre-World War I salon photograph, which showed, through a romantic haze, a remote and lovely lady leaning on a chair and pensively clutching a crystal globe to her chest. De Meyer smartened the lady's attire, surrounded her with a clutter of fashionable decor and replaced the globe with a fan or a vase, and *voila!* the *Vogue* fashion picture was born.

In introducing Modern Photography to *Vogue,* Steichen never got rid of the delicious air of unreality that enveloped the De Meyer lady. However, he sharpened the focus and cleared out the clutter. In the '20s he replaced the moonlight, flowers and 18th and 19th Century vases and tables that surrounded De Meyer's girls with sleek Art Deco objects; by 1930 he was photographing models against severe modernistic backgrounds of gray, black, and white panels, with strongly contrasted lights and shadows. In portraiture he effected similar changes. He abolished the natural lighting, the soft focus and the atmospheric effects of his pre-World War I portraits. In their place he developed a modern portrait style ideally suited to the requirements of magazine reproduction, striving for sharp outlines, bold simplifications, and vivid if artificial contrasts of dark and light.

With this approach the high style of Thirties photography had arrived, and in certain essentials it has never been superseded. Its emphasis on sharpness and clarity (which it shared with documentary photography and photojournalism) has remained the basis of magazine photography ever since. Its tendency to idealize ordinary things—a viewpoint fashion photography inherited from the Pictorialism of the salons—proved equally influential and long lasting. "The alluring photographs, particularly in *Vogue,*" wrote Phyllis Lee Levin in *The Wheels of Fashion,* "changed the look and content of all types of advertising so that automobiles, razors and beans have acquired the glamorous aura once exuded only by women in beautiful clothes."

Steichen was roundly attacked by critics and art photographers for the part he played in this development. In their view advertising and fashion photographers were hacks whose talents were prostituted to selling goods. This adverse judgment was accepted, however reluctantly, even by many advertising professionals who spoke of their work in a tone that wavered uncertainly between apologies and boasts.

Today apologies seem unnecessary. If an authentic expression of an age makes a work of art, the high-style fashion and advertising photographs of the '30s are as truly artistic as the soberer and more realistic works of the documentarians and photojournalists. The only difference is that they expressed the decade's dreams rather than its realities. The '30s was the last decade in which glamor was truly untouched by the ordinary life with which it coexisted. It is this aspect of the era that is epitomized in the Thirties Style introduced by Steichen and fully developed by three of his followers, George Hoyningen-Huene, Cecil Beaton, and Horst.

George Hoyningen-Huene was a Russian baron who became a fashion illustrator after fleeing the Revolution. He was always more interested in clothes and the women who wore them than in the techniques of photography. In fashion photography he accepted Steichen's innovations and proceeded to create within them a cool and elegant world of classical beau-

Industrial photography, influenced no less than fashion and portraiture by the art movements of the '30s, took on an intellectually cool and aristocratic abstraction in the pioneering work of Margaret Bourke-White for FORTUNE. In photographing the Bayonne Bridge (top), a then newly completed link between New Jersey and Staten Island, New York, she transformed concrete and steel into a delicate tracery. Even more abstract is her picture of an inspector checking newly manufactured paper (bottom).

MARGARET BOURKE-WHITE: *Bayonne Bridge*, 1933

MARGARET BOURKE-WHITE: *Oxford Paper, Rumford, Maine*, 1932

ty. A *Vogue* photographer from 1927 to 1934 (when he left to join *Harper's Bazaar),* he photographed most of the artistic and fashionable celebrities of the period. From Elsa Maxwell and Carole Lombard to Igor Stravinsky and members of the Ballet Russe de Monte Carlo, they were self-possessed far beyond the dreams of ordinary humanity. In none of his pictures is there a hint of world-wide depression and the approach of World War II.

Cecil Beaton was warmer and more theatrical. Without abandoning the sharply focused realism of Modern Photography, he revived the artificial decor of Baron de Meyer's Pictorialism, giving it what today would be called a campy twist. He posed his models in grottoes of flowers or against backgrounds of polka-dot cottons. He combed the antique shops of Manhattan for rococo props. He posed high-fashion models in the ruins of abandoned buildings or amid the piles of mortar and brick of office buildings under construction. In Beaton's photographs the intrusion of such bits of everyday reality merely heightened the fantasy mood and set a precedent for many later incursions into dreamland.

Compared to Cecil Beaton, the young German photographer who called himself simply Horst was sobriety itself. A master of studio lighting, he was fired by Condé Nast for daring to suggest that a snip of a boy like himself might someday be as good as Steichen; three months later *Vogue* asked him to come back. Of all the Thirties Style photographers, he was perhaps closest in dramatic elegance to Steichen, although his work had a rococo grace and ease all its own.

At its purest the Thirties Style was a studio creation as artificial as the fantasies painted for the aristocracy of 18th Century Europe by such artists as Boucher and Tiepolo. Their rosy-kneed nymphs and airborne goddesses did not correspond to anything in the real world, certainly not to anything in the restless, troubled world of the final decades of the *ancien régime.* They did, however, perfectly express the dreams and aspirations of the ruling princes and prelates. Spread about in murals on the walls and ceilings of palaces, they gave visible embodiment to the love of pleasure and the dreams of ancestral glory that were soon to perish in the fires of revolution.

By the 1930s mural painting was mainly devoted to edifying celebrations of public virtue such as the Benefits of Industry or the Rise of the Common Man. The decade's private dreams of splendor and opulence were embodied in Hollywood movies or the pages of magazines. The gifted artists who realized those dreams worked, like Boucher and Tiepolo, not for themselves but for others. They were even involved in the sordid selling of goods. But the dreams they expressed were none the less real for that, and the intelligence and artistry of such artists enable us to dream those dreams again today.

A Spell of Glamor

The highly theatrical glamor of the '30s lives on perhaps only in revivals of Hollywood movies and in the photographs of George Hoyningen-Huene, Horst and Cecil Beaton. The portraits and fashion illustrations of these three men, featured in New York gallery exhibitions in 1974, epitomize the photographer's ability to conjure the spare but opulent elegance that characterizes the fantasy world of the '30s. Their work follows Edward Steichen's sharply focused, clear and uncluttered pattern *(page 157),* but each of them brought to the Thirties Style something uniquely his own.

Hoyningen-Huene brought the fanatical devotion and the sure taste of a born aristocrat. The son of a Russian baron and an American diplomat's daughter, he turned to fashion photography after fleeing the 1917 revolution. His love of classical antiquity and his old-fashioned idealization of femininity resulted in pictures of delicate beauty, and he controlled lighting to make the most of dramatic contrasts *(opposite).*

Horst, who grew up amid the poverty and disorder of defeated Germany after World War I, came to photography from architecture, and during the '30s he was virtually the court photographer to the international high society that centered on Paris. He was admired for his theatrical use of lighting—despite the demurrers of fashion editors, who complained that some of his shots were so dark and murky they could not see the dresses.

Cecil Beaton's long career as a designer of sets and costumes for the theater is reflected in the dramatic staging of his fashion photographs, creating effects worthy of Broadway musicals or Hollywood spectaculars. He often took his pictures against large transparent screens of stretched white muslin to produce fantastic shadow shapes.

Fashion photography in the '30s was an art of the studio, in which every effect was carefully manipulated and controlled. The photographer composed his picture on the ground-glass screen of a large (8-by-10-inch) view camera. He had banks of floodlights at his disposal to produce any lighting effect he wanted. He was assisted—and at times impeded—by a horde of editors, stylists, electricians, make-up artists and hairdressers, who could transform a rich society lady or a possibly bedraggled professional model into a fairy-tale princess. Then, when all was arranged to the photographer's satisfaction, someone (not necessarily the photographer himself) tripped the shutter, and glamor materialized.

The American entertainer Josephine Baker, a star of the Folies Bergère in Paris, was at the height of her fame in the '30s and a favorite with photographers for her svelte, exotic beauty. This picture, first published in Vanity Fair in 1931, capitalizes on the '30s photographers' predilection for dramatic lighting, with strong contrast between a giant white feather fan and the simple, dark background of the studio.

GEORGE HOYNINGEN-HUENE: *Josephine Baker*, 1931

The German actor and director Gustaf Gründgens, illuminated by a strong light from below, takes on a personal resemblance to his most celebrated stage role, Mephistopheles in Goethe's Faust. Vertical lines link the image to the background in the manner of contemporary abstract art.

GEORGE HOYNINGEN-HUENE: *Gustaf Gründgens*, 1932

GEORGE HOYNINGEN-HUENE: *Madame Muñoz,* 1933

Madame Alvarez Muñoz, wife of a Spanish diplomat, was one of many society women who modeled for fashion photographers in the '30s. She was, according to Vogue, "one of that small handful of Continentals who influence the clothes of the world." Artfully lit and smiling ever so faintly, she here wears a hat by Caroline Reboux, the milliner then the darling of the couture.

GEORGE HOYNINGEN-HUENE: *Suzette Salen*, 1932

In a setting that establishes the cool fantasy of elegance marking the photographic style of the '30s, a Vionnet gown is modeled by Suzette Salen, the favorite model of Hoyningen-Huene. The background was created by Jean-Michel Frank, then one of the most influential interior designers in Paris. Its parchment-covered panels and inlaid commode are typical of the '30s Art Deco style.

GEORGE HOYNINGEN-HUENE: *Alix gown, 1936*

The Grecian look of this dress was partly the work of the designer, Madame Grès, who in the '30s worked under the name Alix. But it was also the work of the photographer, who posed the model and lit the scene to bring out the classical lines. More than any other photographer of the day, Hoyningen-Huene emphasized the pervasive neoclassicism of the Thirties Style.

GEORGE HOYNINGEN-HUENE: *The Duke of Windsor,* 1937

This portrait of a pensive Duke of Windsor at the time of his marriage to the American divorcee Wallis Warfield Simpson was one of several taken by Hoyningen-Huene for Harper's Bazaar. The picture actually published in the magazine was a more pompous and conventional three-quarter view that gave a better idea of what the 42-year-old bridegroom actually looked like. Here, however, a romantic note is struck by silhouetting, which suppresses details and casts a cloud of sadness over the Duke's boyish good looks.

Baron Nicolas de Gunzburg was one of the leaders of the cosmopolitan society that centered in Paris in the '30s. In this portrait by Horst he is dressed up as an Austrian archduke of the 1860s for a 1934 costume ball. Horst's romantic feeling for 19th Century subjects is evident in this picture, which was taken in a studio before the ball with rented sculptures as props.

HORST: *Baron de Gunzburg,* 1934

HORST: *Fashion and jewelry, 1938*

The girl (Estrella Boissevain), the hat (a smart little Breton straw by Reboux) and the dress (pleated white crepe from Saks Fifth Avenue) are all featured in this unusual picture within a picture taken for Vogue in 1938. However, star billing goes to the diamonds and pearls from Cartier, shown both on the model and scattered like offerings on the table in front of her picture. The bracelet in the foreground is lit from both sides to enhance the effect of radiant glitter, roundness and luminosity.

HORST: *Piguet suit, 1936*

Horst's preoccupation with dramatic lighting
effects was the despair of fashion editors, who
complained that in his so-called ''black''
pictures they could not see the details of the
clothes. In this brilliant example of his ''black''
style, the felt hat is by Talbot and the wool
suit by Piguet, both well-known Paris designers
of the '30s. But what Horst cared about was
the contrast between the brightly lighted sleeve
and the silhouette of the hat and dress.

CECIL BEATON: *Shadow Her*, 1935

Mysterious shadows of men turn what would otherwise have been a routine fashion picture into a spectacle worthy of a Busby Berkeley movie.

The Luxury of Color

Color photography is now a familiar feature of most major magazines, but in the '30s, when it first began to be used extensively, it appeared mostly on the advertising pages. One of the pioneers was Nickolas Muray, whose 40 years of portrait and advertising photography was the subject of a 1974 exhibition at the International Museum of Photography in Rochester, New York. Muray was a Hungarian commercial lithographer and photoengraver who immigrated to America at the beginning of World War I. In the '20s he set himself up in New York as a portrait photographer, and his pictures appeared in *Harper's Bazaar, Vanity Fair,* the *Ladies' Home Journal* and *McCall's.* In the '30s he began to specialize in full-color advertising photography.

Muray was a master of the carbro process, still used occasionally to make high-quality color prints but then the principal means of preparing color photographs for reproduction in magazines. Muray did not start out using color film—the first of the modern types became available only in 1935. Instead he had to make three black-and-white negatives with three different color filters, producing "separation negatives" that recorded primary colors as shades of gray. An expensive and complex "one-shot" camera was required. It had only one lens, but inside an arrangement of mirrors split the light from the subject three ways so that all three of the negatives were made simultaneously. The three black-and-white negatives were then converted into three translucent layers of dyed gelatin, which were carefully mounted in register on an opaque white backing to make the print.

The first carbro-process color advertisement that Nickolas Muray made appeared in the *Ladies' Home Journal* in 1931—a picture of 17 girls in bathing suits beside a hotel pool in Miami Beach. He developed the technique to a fine art, and went on to produce carbro color advertisements for many of the largest corporations.

In one important respect Muray's carbro color work differed from the high-style black-and-white photography of the '30s. Photographers who worked in black and white used strong contrasts of light and shadow to build up drama and tension on the printed page. Color photographers like Muray preferred a more generalized lighting that enabled the color itself to play a major part in the picture. As Muray said, "Color calls for a new way of looking at people, at things, *and* a new way of looking at color."

This photograph of a fashionably dressed lady was made by the carbro color-print method for a cigarette advertisement in 1936. Overall, the colors are rich but muted. However, bright scarlet splashes on the lady's lips and on the chair just behind the hand holding the cigarette accent the main subject of the picture, which otherwise might be taken for a fashion illustration or a portrait of a rich society lady.

NICKOLAS MURAY: *Cigarette advertisement,* 1936

In 1933 readers of FORTUNE, The Saturday
Evening Post, Ladies' Home Journal and Motor
Life saw automobile ads like this one. The
situation is basically absurd: a society lady
appears to have driven into the palm-fringed
lobby of a luxury hotel. However, the allure
of the automobile is suggested by the opulent
setting and costumes and the soft colors
that Nickolas Muray characteristically obtained
from the complex color prints he produced.

NICKOLAS MURAY: *Automobile advertisement,* 1933

Two famous movie stars of the '30s, Fredric March and Claudette Colbert, take the pause that refreshes on a California patio in this 1933 advertising photograph. The full-color realism of such pictures stood out among the drawn and painted illustrations then prevalent in magazines. Lithographed cutouts made from the photographs were given to soda fountains for display; they now sell to collectors for as much as $1,000.

NICKOLAS MURAY: *Soft-drink advertisement, 1933*

The Annual Awards /6

The Annual Awards/6

A Diverse World   184

Photographer of the Year—U.S.A.
*Under the bulb-studded folds of an electric
Old Glory, a grinning President Nixon accepts
adulation from a Washington, D.C. audience
whom he has just assured he would not quit under
fire. The White House News Photographers
awarded McNamee their top prize long before the
President's resignation made the picture ironic.*

WALLY McNAMEE: *"I'm not a crook"* 1973

The Annual Awards

A Diverse World in Photographs

In an age of instant communications and fading cultural differences, the year's best-picture awards offer a refreshing reminder that regional variations still persist

Though regional and national idiosyncrasies may be disappearing under the pressures of satellite television, movies, transistor radios and jet travel, the appeal of a familiar local image, even when it reflects a cliché, is strong enough to provoke a chuckle, stimulate thought—or win an award. Accordingly, wise truths and easy stereotypes about national identity and culture are woven through the major photography prizes of 1974. Where else but in the United States could you find a mammoth electric Stars and Stripes with hundreds of lights beaming from its rigid furls? Gina Lollobrigida's photograph of a girl and girl watchers *(page 192)* immediately says Italy.

Such pictures—humorous, wry, or blunt—were comments on the truism that clichés are rooted in the actuality of life. But photographers were also rewarded for their ability to capture on film that special sensitivity that develops when a person from one culture looks closely and carefully at another. An Italian photographer who traveled to China subtly evoked his western image of that ancient and complex society: a lone man dwarfed by the massive steps of the Peking Summer Palace *(page 186)*. And a Japanese photographer mirrored the immobile and static grandeur of ancient Egypt in a stylized contemporary photograph *(page 191)*.

Indeed, the most distinctive and profound cultural stamp is on the work of the Japanese photographers. The scope of their pictures was often as narrow as an inventory of images of a single small mountain range or a painstaking study of the design of traditional Japanese storehouses. But each of the five Japanese winners produced patient, ardent, book-length documentations of the world they examined. Form, an awareness of tradition, and a passion for detail mark the photographs.

The criteria for granting awards to such pictures are, of course, primarily artistic. Where the criterion is news (as in the two Pulitzers), or the valor of the photographer (the Robert Capa Gold Medal), the common denominator of the prize-winning photographs is often violence. In 1974, however, even these pictures convey the diversity of national character. Only in America, perhaps, could a grotesque and tragic drama of attempted kidnapping and sudden death be played out between the cars of a shopping center parking lot *(page 199)*. And the pictures that reported the toppling of Salvador Allende's regime in Chile—and the country's ruthless takeover by a military junta *(pages 194-196)*—reinforce a popular image of Latin American politics as unstable and undemocratic.

Magazine Photographer of the Year—U.S.A.

Arkansas teenagers frolic boisterously in an archetypal rural scene from the National Geographic's book "American Mountain People." The School of Journalism at the University of Missouri, the National Press Photographers Association and Nikon, Inc., sponsored this award and the ones on pages 186 and 197.

BRUCE DALE: *Swimming hole,* 1973

World Understanding Award—U.S.A.

A solitary Chinese enveloped in his sheepskin coat descends an immense staircase of the Summer Palace near Peking. The Japanese Nikon corporation joined the University of Missouri and the National Press Photographers Association of the United States in granting this top prize to an Italian.

GIORGIO LOTTI: *Man on stairs,* 1973

Sharp metal edges menace the rounded contours of a gilded nude in this unsettling photographic contrast of flesh and gleaming metal sculpture. The photographer is a restaurateur with a taste for audacious experiments in color photography.

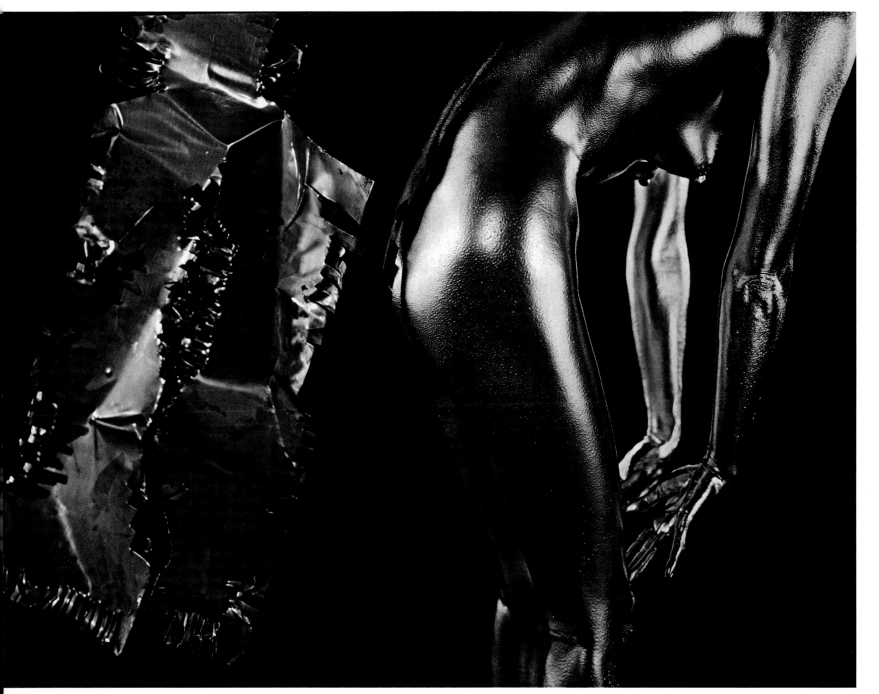

KEIICHIRO GOTO: *Copper and gold*, 1973

Nendo Sho (Annual Award)—Japan

*Near a snowfield on the slope of a mountain in
northern Japan, clumps of new green leaves
thrust up from a tangle of dead winter grasses.
The prize-winning photographer, who lives near
this small range of mountains, has concentrated
for 18 years on capturing fragile moments
such as this seasonal metamorphosis.*

YOSHIHIKO SHIGA: *Spring,* 1972

**Shinjin Sho (Newcomer Award)
—Japan**

*Trees, stone and architecture intersect in
an austere composition of the storehouses
for supplies and ornaments built atop the
walls of a 300-year-old castle. Through
documentation of hundreds of traditional
kura, or storehouses—some dating as far
back as the Third Century B.C.—the
photographer has preserved the images of
structures that are fast disappearing.*

KIYOSHI TAKAI: *Kumamoto castle,* 1972

Shinjin Sho (Newcomer Award)—Japan

*Sheltering a three-stringed instrument under
her oiled-paper cape on a rainy autumn day,
an old blind woman plays and sings outside a
village house in northern Japan. Brought
up in the area, the photographer remembered
these traditional rural entertainers from boyhood
and returned to record their harsh life.*

TERUTAKA HASHIMOTO: *Goze woman*, 1972

Nendo Sho (Annual Award)—Japan

*In a technically sophisticated study of receding
vertical forms, this photograph taken on the east
bank of the Nile provides a haunting glimpse
of the past—with classic temple columns, palm
trees and a timeless Egyptian family (center).
The Japanese photographer's prize-winning book
"Eternal Egypt" resulted from six trips
to Egypt over a period of a dozen years.*

YUKICHI WATABE: *Temple and palms,* 1962

GINA LOLLOBRIGIDA: *Rome. The Spanish Steps*, 1971

Le Prix Niepce—France

A sophisticated variation on a naïve tourist cliché, this whimsical image of a priest kneeling to take a picture of a group of nuns at the 14th Century papal residence in Avignon helped a newcomer to photography win a top award.

Le Prix Nadar—France

Reacting to stares and whistles with blithe good humor, a stylishly dressed young woman strides past lounging males. To avoid recognition —and the certainty of similar treatment—the famed actress-photographer who took the picture donned wigs, glasses and jeans on a tour of her native country for her book,"Italia Mia."

PIERRE MICHAUD: *Avignon—Palace of the Popes,* 1973

Robert Capa Gold Medal—U.S.A.

Photographed during the first days of agrarian reforms instituted in 1971 by Chile's Marxist President Salvador Allende, Chilean peasants show their ancient rural skepticism. The photographer shared the award with two others (below and opposite), who recorded the Allende government's collapse two years later.

RAYMOND DEPARDON: *Three peasants*, 1971

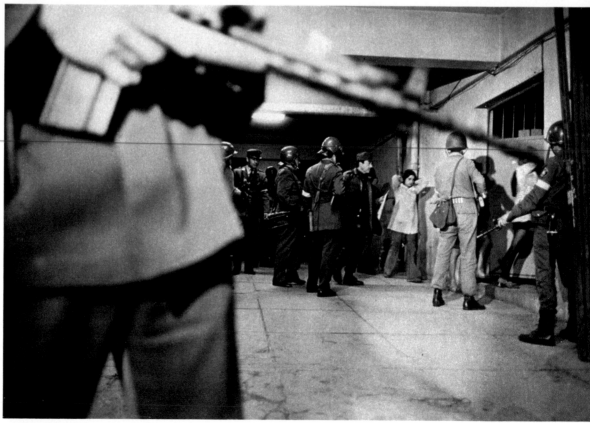

After Allende's overthrow and death in 1973, heavily armed soldiers and officers march young women supporters of the late President into Santiago's National Stadium, converted to a prison. The 27-year-old American photographer was arrested soon after he took this picture, and all but one roll of his film confiscated.

DAVID BURNETT: *The National Stadium*, 1973

CHAS GERRETSEN: *Masked soldiers*, 1973

During the attack by the insurgent army on Chile's presidential palace, Dutch photographer Chas Gerretsen risked sniper fire from die-hard Allende defenders inside the palace to get close to four soldiers, masked against the fumes of their own tear gas and huddling behind a tank.

**Press Photo of the Year Award—
The Netherlands**

*In another prize-winning picture that
emerged from the Chilean crisis, President
Allende—clad in turtleneck and helmet,
and carrying a rifle—checks the defenses of
his palace with armed aides only hours
before his death. The photographer, a former
member of Allende's staff, has remained
anonymous in order to continue living in Chile.*

PHOTOGRAPHER UNKNOWN: *President Allende's last day, 1973*

Newspaper Photographer of the Year
—U.S.A.

*On an Indiana main street, a newsboy stares
incredulously at the hooded figure of a Ku Klux
Klansman, in town for a rare Klan reunion.
The boy's lack of recognition reflects profound
changes in rural Indiana, once a stronghold
of the Klan. The organization has long
since moved elsewhere or gone underground.*

RON SMITH: *Are you for real?* 1973

**Pulitzer Prize for
Feature Photography—U.S.A.**
*Half a decade of pent-up longing explodes from
this single frame as the family of Air Force
Lieutenant Colonel Robert Stirm rush across an
airport runway to greet him on his return after
his years in a North Vietnamese prison.*

SAL VEDER: *Burst of Joy,* 1973

Pulitzer Prize for
Spot News Photography—U.S.A.

*From behind a car, a security guard aims his
pistol at a man he has caught holding a woman
on the ground. In the second picture, the
man uses his victim as a shield. After reacting
to this with a single accurate shot into
the assailant's brain, the guard is shown—in
the third frame—holding the gun aloft to
prevent a second, accidental shot in the
crowded lot. At bottom, the assailant lies dead.*

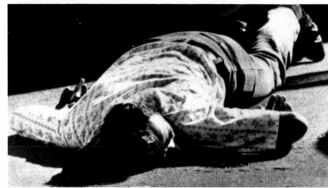

ANTHONY K. ROBERTS: *Hollywood violence,* 1973

Sports Photographer of the Year—
Great Britain

*Dancing and howling with the pain of
a dislocated finger, a Polish goalie stops
the action during the qualifying round
of the World Cup soccer matches at Wembley
Stadium, near London. As a doctor tries to treat
him, the player's teammates, accustomed to
injuries on the field, look on with dispassion.*

PETER JAY: *Tomaszewski's agony,* 1973

The Year's Books / 7

Doisneau's Paris / ROBERT DOISNEAU: *Old couple, 1953, and Centaur, 1971 (a print made from two negatives)*

Doisneau's Love Affair with Paris

With a flair for memorable juxtapositions, a French photographer captures modern Parisians against the ornate face of their aging city

LE PARIS DE ROBERT DOISNEAU ET MAX-POL FOUCHET
Photographs by Robert Doisneau. Text by Max-Pol Fouchet. 192 pages. Les Editeurs Français Réunis, Paris, 1974. 110 francs (about $23).

Paris is home to Robert Doisneau. It is also his joy, his obsession, and almost the sole focus of his art. Since the late 1920s, the 62-year-old Frenchman—a onetime engraver, label designer and commercial photographer—has been prowling the boulevards and alleyways of France's capital, seeking the bizarre, the poignant, the ironic and, above all, the uniquely Parisian. Completely familiar with Paris street life, Doisneau moves unobtrusively among shopkeepers, window-shoppers, laborers, and school children, to capture in photographs present-day life in a very old city. The resulting juxtapositions of old and new are not only characteristic of Paris itself, but are also trademarks of Doisneau's photography. His work has appeared in major magazines on three continents and in a number of books, most of them published only in his native land.

In 1968 Doisneau learned that the administration of Charles de Gaulle had decided to demolish entire sections of Paris and rebuild them along functional, modern lines; the photographer decided to make a record of the doomed neighborhoods, their architecture and street life. Day and night he scoured the city, focusing his 35mm camera on delicately etched café windows, tiled store fronts and other reminders of a simpler age that were scheduled for the wrecker's ball. At first unable to find a publisher for this testament to a vanishing era, Doisneau accepted an editor's suggestion; he broadened his scope to include pictures of people who live—often totally unaware of the evocative beauty of their surroundings—among the statues, architecture and ornaments that gave the city its unmistakable ambience.

Le Paris de Robert Doisneau et Max-Pol Fouchet is the result of Doisneau's efforts—in collaboration with Fouchet, a popular French critic who provided the text. Unfortunately, only a small number of people will have the opportunity of seeing the entire work, which is published solely in a French edition limited to 4,000 copies, each selling for 110 francs (about $23). This is a great pity, for few photographers show such adeptness at capturing the elemental Paris. In Doisneau's *Le Paris,* the City of Light is portrayed with a tender humor tinged with regret, a gentle melancholy that mourns the languid, slowly disappearing past and warns of a homogenized future.

Indeed, that future is—to some degree—already the present. For although the vast majority of the pictures in *Le Paris* were taken in the late 1960s and early 1970s, fully three quarters of the buildings shown have since been torn down in the name of progress. The fright-mask entrance to the night club L'Enfer in the Montmartre section of the city *(opposite)* has long since vanished and, more recently, the café with the etched window *(page 206)* was also demolished. But despite the inroads made by steel, plastic, and machines, Paris—through the eyes of Doisneau—remains a city apart: a place of individuals who have not yet yielded to the anonymity of mass culture.

A Paris policeman strolls past the gaping maw that formed the entrance to an abandoned night spot, L'Enfer (Hell). Popular around 1900, L'Enfer closed during World War II; in the early days the cabaret had a neighborhood competitor called Le Ciel (Heaven).

Waiting in a café, 1971

The flowing lines of an etched-glass café window evoke an age of lost elegance; in vivid contrast, the crash helmets in front of a bored Parisian woman awaiting her motorcycling companion tell of a Paris metamorphosed by speed and noise, a city that only rarely pauses to contemplate its past.

The statue of a woman, part of a monument honoring French writer Guy de Maupassant, appears in this photograph to be a reluctant baby-sitter studiously ignoring three youngsters out for an autumn stroll through Paris's fashionable Parc Monceau. Doisneau often treats the city's monuments as if they were living figures to be satirized.

In the Parc Monceau, 1971

*Their forms begrimed by pigeon droppings,
their classic calm assailed by the chatter
of helicopters, Maillol's Les Nymphes defy the
insults of nature and the obtrusiveness of man
to retain all the grace with which their
sculptor endowed them. Doisneau was watching
a Bastille Day display from the Tuileries
Gardens when the helicopters appeared overhead.*

Statues and helicopters, 1972

In the Place du Carrousel, 1971

In a busy Paris square, Doisneau placed his
camera on a low tripod to juxtapose the graceful
curves of a mini-skirted leg and a stylized
dolphin on the base of a street lamp. In the
resulting photograph the dolphin grins in
approval of the oblivious walker.

In front of a dairy store, 1971

Lost in thought, a young Parisian at the entrance of the Paramount movie house seems unaware of the giant female gunslinger guarding the theater. "Little dramas of everyday life" are basic source material for Doisneau's art.

A boy dashing home with a bottle of milk ignores the farm girl on a tiled shop façade. Such juxtapositions express one of Doisneau's favorite themes: the contrast of fast-paced Parisian life with symbols of a more leisurely time.

At the Paramount, 1972

211

Penn's Travels in a Small Room

A great fashion photographer, carrying his studio with him, pursues the unexpected

WORLDS IN A SMALL ROOM
By Irving Penn. 95 pages. Grossman
Publishers, New York, 1974. $16.50.

For fashion photographer Irving Penn, *Worlds in a Small Room,* his first book in 14 years, is primarily the result of a pilgrimage, though it also represents a diversion from a career spent beneath the artificial lights of a Manhattan studio. As a young photographer, long before his fashion photographs and portraits became the elegant trademark of one of America's leading fashion magazines, *Vogue,* Penn deplored the confinement of the studio. "I would often find myself daydreaming," he writes in his introduction to *Small Room,* "of being mysteriously deposited (with my ideal north-light studio) among the disappearing aborigines in remote parts of the earth." One dividend of becoming a successful photographer is the chance to make such dreams a reality. Set down over a period of 23 years, *Worlds in a Small Room* is Penn's photographic record, in black and white, of his journeys on five continents to find and photograph the peoples he had dreamed about. The photographs on the following pages are taken from the African chapters of the book. Most of Penn's traveling was done for *Vogue,* which published selected photographs from the trips, but many of the pictures appear for the first time in the book.

As Penn journeyed from the port cities of the sub-Sahara to the foothills of the Himalayas, he found not only the pre-industrial subjects of his dreams but something else he missed inside a New York studio: the north light beloved by painters and photographers alike. "There is a sweetness and constancy to light that falls into a studio from the north sky," Penn says, "that sets it beyond any other illumination."

While on the road, Penn depended on his ingenuity to find suitable shooting locations. In Cuzco, Peru, he rented a daylight studio to make his portraits of Peruvian Indians, and in Crete he found two storage buildings open to north light. In 1967, for his first African trip, Penn decided to construct a studio that he could transport with him in rented Land Rovers or Jeeps. This portable studio, the "small room" of the book's title, is a rectangular nylon tent with one side completely open to the light and a painted gray canvas background hanging inside. Whether his studio was improvised or packaged, Penn's principle was always the same: to pose human beings against a neutral background and allow north light to bathe them in its sweetness.

Although Penn was naturally influenced by the postures and backdrops of fashion photography, there was another reason why he chose to handle his subjects as he did. By photographing Arab market women outside their market, a Berber shepherd girl without her flock, Penn eliminated the carnival quality that so often degrades photographs of the world's exotic people. Instead, a superb portrait photographer has isolated his subjects and allowed them to be seen as human beings.

Penn's 11-by-20-foot portable studio, stationed here on a Nepalese stream bed, can be folded up into a 13-by-32-inch package. The studio can be positioned so that one side admits Penn's favored north light.

Three Arab market women, Morocco, 1971

Man and woman of the Guider tribe, Cameroon, 1969

A young Berber shepherdess, Morocco, 1971

Cartier-Bresson's Return to Russia

On a new visit, the mellowing master catches moments more warm than decisive

ABOUT RUSSIA
By Henri Cartier-Bresson. 180 pages. Studio Books/
The Viking Press, New York, 1974. $18.95.

Whenever a book by France's Henri Cartier-Bresson appears, it stirs excite ment among photography enthusiasts. For more than four decades, Cartier Bresson, 35mm camera in hand, has traveled the world to produce suc remarkable books as *The Europeans* and *The Decisive Moment*. His picture have been exhibited in innumerable galleries and museums, and he has fou times received the Overseas Press Club award for the best photographic re porting from abroad: in 1949, for his coverage of Gandhi's funeral, and for hi essays on Russia in 1955, China in 1960, and Cuba in 1964. In his latest book *About Russia,* Cartier-Bresson has brought back a stunning report from tw trips to the Soviet Union in 1972-1973. The book is a selective photographi tour from the Arctic wastes of Siberia (where Cartier-Bresson's film froze i the 40°-below-zero temperatures) to the relatively civilized pleasures c Leningrad and Moscow.

The distinction of Cartier-Bresson's pictures has long been his uncann ability to grasp—totally and instantly—the way his subjects confront thei environment and their condition. Such "decisive moments" of pain, joy, love and hate are universal, and in them all men may see their own images. Thi work appears almost two decades after the photographer's first book, *The People of Moscow,* based on his earlier trip to the Soviet Union; it reveals a changed Russia and a different Cartier-Bresson. Here Soviet citizens ar shown in the course of their everyday activities, their minds apparently les occupied than formerly by ideology. Workers in a steel mill spend a momen chatting, a May Day celebration is observed with bicycle races, Russian fash ion models strike stylized poses in the best capitalist tradition, and sailor ashore flirt with a young, admiring woman.

About Russia reflects a certain relaxation in Soviet society born of détent and prosperity. But it may also represent a relaxation in Cartier-Bresson' eye. No longer does the decisive moment appear uppermost in the photog rapher's consciousness; instead, his pictures reveal a mellowed attitude— what might be called the "continuing moment"—which allows life's norma rhythms, as well as its peaks, to convey their meanings.

While in Moscow, Cartier-Bresson met with a group of more than 100 Rus sian photographers, who treated him with a respect bordering on awe and questioned him about his work. "Photography is only intuition," he told them "a perpetual interrogation—everything except a stage set." It is precisel these qualities—intuitive feeling, curiosity, lack of artifice—that make *Abou Russia* the work of a master.

Against a background of giant machines, workers in an iron-and-steel complex in the Caucasus pause t talk. In their purposeful faces, Cartier-Bresson catches much of the energy of Soviet industrializatior

Washerwomen by the Kamenka River at Suzdal

In a scene evocative of times long past, Russian women, bundled against a fierce November wind, do their wash in the icy Kamenka River of Suzdal. In the background is the medieval city, with its onion-domed kremlin—a citadel built during the 11th and 12th centuries.

Russian models in the new season's finery work with a photographer, their setting the vast forecourt of the Hermitage Palace in Leningrad. Behind the models a towering cutout of Lenin, father of the Soviet Union, appears to stride purposefully toward the women as if to put a stop to such bourgeois frippery.

Models in Hermitage Square, Leningrad

On a cooperative farm near Yaroslavl on the Volga River a little girl hurries along a fence-bordered country path beneath a profusion of spring blossoms. The freshly painted cottage behind her, its intricate wood scrollwork spick and span, is a sign of prosperity—as is the plump chicken in the foreground.

cooperative farm near Yaroslavl

May Day bicycle race in Tallinn

A cyclist in a May Day race through the ancient city of Tallinn, capital of the Soviet Union's Estonian Republic, strains to maintain speed on a cobblestone street. In spite of his effort, the spectators appear far more interested in the progress of an off-camera rival—perhaps a hometown favorite starting his bid for victory.

Soviet sailors enjoy a flirtatious moment in Leningrad during a May 9th celebration of Russia's World War II victory over Germany. During the war, the city was besieged for more than two years; tens of thousands starved to death, and Leningrad, festive on the day shown here, was then strewn with corpses.

Sailors in Palace Square, Leningrad

Ansel Adams: A Half Century of Images

A craftsman famed for his majestic panoramas reveals a superb insight into human personality

ANSEL ADAMS: IMAGES 1923-1974
Foreword by Wallace Stegner. 128 pages.
New York Graphic Society, Boston, 1974. $75.00.

In 1974 the photography world threw Ansel Adams a joyous, year-long party. He received an honorary doctorate from the University of Massachusetts, and his intensely American work was celebrated outside the country: he traveled to France as the honored guest of the art festival at Arles. But the most valuable gifts he received were two thoughtful and acute retrospectives: a show at The Metropolitan Museum of Art in April, which was the photographer's first one-man show in a New York City museum, and a splendidly produced book entitled *Ansel Adams: Images 1923-1974.*

Like some Biblical patriarch, the 73-year-old Adams still treks through the wilderness of North America, relentlessly seeking the most awesome vistas. At times he spends hours waiting for the light to transform a mountain range. Most often, however, he stops and shoots each picture as he sees it, without elaborate preparation. "If I wait too long, I may be losing something else," he explains. Over the past five decades he has recorded powerful landscapes on film so regularly, and the Sierra Club posters of his works have become so familiar, that the titanic prospects no longer awe the viewer. The repetition of Adams's striking, unpopulated panoramas seems overly theatrical to some. Critics have begun to complain that they are more grandiose than grand.

But the 120 photographs reproduced in *Images* reveal that Adams can grip the observer with great subtlety as well as great power. A master of the tonal qualities of black-and-white film, he manipulates the full range of light and shadow to convey the mystery of wild places—as well as their drama. The Grand Teton peak standing guard, like a stronghold of Wagnerian Valkyries at a bend in the Snake River is an Adams hallmark. But his rock-curtained cliffs at Kawoah Gap in the Sierra, delicately shrouding a passageway to the unknown, are a surprise. Equally startling is the knowing intimacy of the portraits in *Images.* Painter Georgia O'Keeffe, ordinarily seen as a lady of regal dignity, is caught by Adams with a sassy expression, apparently flirting with a shy or bemused cowboy, Orville Cox; stormy clouds rushing past the pair's heads add the classic Adams signature. Even a portrait taken indoors expresses Adams's larger-than-life vision of man and nature. The photograph of Adams's painter friend Gottardo Piazzoni, for example, isolates the artist and his work in a lonely moment of creativity in his San Francisco studio. In pictures like these, *Images* secures Adams's reputation by convincing the viewer that both the vistas and the portraits are genuinely awesome, not falsely heroic.

Teton Range and the Snake River, Grand Teton National Park, Wyoming, 1942

Shooting directly into the late afternoon sun, which is partially hidden by storm clouds gathering over Wyoming's Teton mountains, Adams transforms a bend in the Snake River into a vein of raw silver

Georgia O'Keeffe and Orville Cox, Canyon de Chelly National Monument, Arizona, 1937

Frozen Lake and Cliffs, Kaweah Gap, Sequoia National Park, California, 1927

Gottardo Piazzoni in his studio, San Francisco, 1932

Other Books

Of the photography books published in 1974, the editors especially recommend the following:

Current Work

THE BLACK PHOTOGRAPHERS ANNUAL, VOLUME 2
Edited by Joe Crawford. Black Photographers Annual, Inc., Brooklyn, N.Y. 107 pages. Hardbound, $10.95; softbound, $5.95. A collection of the best of 51 photographers from America, Canada and England.

BRIDGES: THE SPANS OF NORTH AMERICA
By David Plowden. A Studio Book/The Viking Press, New York. 328 pages. $27.50. Photographs of bridges great and small.

BUCKS COUNTY
By Aaron Siskind, text by William Morgan. Horizon Press, New York. 112 pages. $12.95. A pictorial record of 17th to 19th Century farmhouses, barns, mills and bridges from the historic Pennsylvania county.

THE CIRCLE OF SEASONS
By Dennis Stock, text by Josephine W. Johnson. A Studio Book/The Viking Press, New York. 104 pages. $16.95. Color photographs of landscapes and animals as they change over the year.

GANGA: SACRED RIVER OF INDIA
By Raghubir Singh, introduction by Eric Newby. The Perennial Press, New York. 158 pages. $30.00. Following the Ganges, from the Himalayas to Calcutta, with a young Indian photographer.

GOODBYE PICASSO
By David Douglas Duncan. Grosset & Dunlap, Inc., New York. 300 pages. $35.00. Intimate glimpses of the famous artist at work and play.

THE MOST NATURAL THING IN THE WORLD
By Leif Skoogfors, text by John Cooney and Lenore Cooney. Harper & Row, New York. Unnumbered pages. $3.95. Photo-reportage of the civil strife in Northern Ireland.

MOTHER EARTH, FATHER SKY
By Marcia Keegan. Grossman Publishers, New York. 112 pages. $16.95. Color photographs of the Navajo and Pueblo Indians.

SON OF BITCH
By Elliot Erwitt, introduction by P. G. Wodehouse. Grossman Publishers, New York. 128 pages. $5.95. A humorous collection of dog photographs.

THIS LIVING REEF
By Douglas Faulkner. Quadrangle/The New York Times Book Co. 184 pages. $27.50. Underwater color photographs from a Micronesian archipelago.

TRAVELOG
By Charles Harbutt. The MIT Press, Cambridge, Mass. Unnumbered pages. Hardbound, $15.00; softbound, $7.95. Faces and scenes, mainly from the cities of the United States and Europe.

THE WAY LIFE WAS
Compiled and written by Jeffrey Simpson. Praeger Publishers, New York. Unnumbered pages. $19.95. A patchwork quilt of scenes of American life at the turn of the century.

Retrospectives

THE DARKNESS AND THE LIGHT: PHOTOGRAPHS BY DORIS ULMANN
Preface by William Clift, afterword by Robert Coles. 111 pages. Aperture, Inc., Millerton, N.Y. $12.50. Portraits, taken from 1918 to 1934, of black people in the rural South.

WILLIAM H. JACKSON
By Beaumont Newhall and Diana E. Edkins. Morgan & Morgan, Inc., Dobbs Ferry, N.Y., in cooperation with the Amon Carter Museum, Fort Worth, Texas. 158 pages. $14.00. Dramatic landscapes and portraits from the 19th Century West.

J'AIME PARIS
By André Kertész, edited by Nicolas Ducrot. Grossman Publishers, New York. 224 pages. $22.50. A tribute to the French city, photographed over four decades.

LES FEMMES
By J. H. Lartigue. E. P. Dutton & Co., Inc., New York. 127 pages. $18.95. A Frenchman's 70-year chronicle of beautiful women.

RALPH EUGENE MEATYARD
Edited by James Baker Hall. Aperture, Inc., Millerton, N.Y. 136 pages. Hardbound, $12.50; softbound, $8.50. Highly original portraits and views by the late American master.

ONE MIND'S EYE
By Arnold Newman. David R. Godine, Boston. Unnumbered pages. $27.50. Portraits of the talented, rich and famous.

PHOTOGRAPHY IN AMERICA
Edited by Robert Doty, introduction by Minor White. A Ridge Press Book/Random House, New York. 255 pages. $25.00. A history in pictures of American photography.

SINGULAR IMAGES
By Ansel Adams. Morgan & Morgan, Inc., Dobbs Ferry, N.Y. Unnumbered pages. $7.50. Landscapes and portraits made by the Polaroid Land process.

Collections

MASTERS OF CONTEMPORARY PHOTOGRAPHY
Prepared by the editors of Alskog, Inc. Thomas Y. Crowell Company, New York. 96 pages per volume. Hardbound, $7.95; softbound, $3.95. A series devoted to contemporary photographers, with a technical section at the back of each volume. Volumes published in 1974: Paul Fusco and Will McBride, "The Photo Essay"; Bert Stern, "The Photo Illustrator"; Mary Ellen Mark and Annie Liebowitz, "The Photojournalist"; Elliot Erwitt, "The Private Experience."

Technical

BIGGER AND BETTER ENLARGING
By Don Nibbelink and Rex Anderson. Amphoto, Garden City, N.Y. 288 pages. $9.95. A lavishly illustrated primer of black-and-white and color printing, with step-by-step instructions.

A CREATIVE APPROACH TO CONTROLLING PHOTOGRAPHY
By Harry Boyd, Jr. Heidelberg Publishers, Inc., Austin, Texas. 289 pages. $12.95. For advanced amateurs and professionals, a guide to manipulating the photographic process in both the camera and the darkroom, with emphasis on special effects.

THE PERFECT PHOTOGRAPH
By Andreas Feininger. Amphoto, Garden City, N.Y. 176 pages. $9.95. What makes a good photograph and suggestions for achieving one. A philosophical view for all photography enthusiasts.

PHOTOGRAPHIC COMPOSITION
By Ben Clements and David Rosenfeld. Prentice-Hall, Inc., Englewood Cliffs, N.J. 260 pages. $10.95. Artistic principles for the serious photographer who wishes to achieve self-expression.

VAN NOSTRAND REINHOLD MANUAL OF PROFESSIONAL PHOTOGRAPHY
By Phillip Gotlop. Van Nostrand Reinhold Company, New York. 208 pages. $9.95. Tools and techniques of photography—ranging from basic definitions to sophisticated applications.

Roundup / 8

Roundup/8

Milestones/IHEI KIMURA: *A gardener raking leaves, Versailles Palace, France,* 1954

Roundup

Milestones

Ihei Kimura 1901-1974

Ihei Kimura, the photojournalist generally given credit for introducing the 35mm camera to Japan, died in May of a heart attack. In a career that spanned half a century, he had developed and, by his example, taught a new style of photography in his native land. Jun Miki, an official of the Japan Photographers' Association, eulogized Kimura as "the great benefactor of modern Japanese photography."

Kimura became intrigued by the miniature camera in 1929. While he was covering a pioneering flight from Germany to Japan, he noticed a German official using a Leica. Though the then-new instrument had been introduced into Japan three years earlier, only a handful had been sold and they were regarded as novelties. Kimura realized that the inconspicuous, fast camera could free him from the stiff, artificial style typical of the 1920s and allow him to photograph everyday occurrences with available light at a moment's notice.

In 1932 Kimura helped found an influential magazine, *Kohga (Light Pictures),* devoted largely to candid photography. In the following year he established his own reputation with his first major exhibition, a one-man show of candid portraits of Japanese authors and poets entitled "Prominent Faces."

Kimura trained his lens on commonplace events and on the lives of everyday people wherever he traveled, both inside and outside Japan. During a 1954 trip through Europe he used a cold November sun to capture a French gardener raking leaves *(page 229).* In the two photographs below, Kimura also concentrated on people at work: a farm woman sifting rice with a traditional bamboo basket on Japan's largest island, Honshu *(below, left),* and three workers picking lint from a carpet in an unheated Peking factory *(below, right).* His sensitivity of observation won for Kimura a number of Japan's highly prized cultural awards and helped influence his countrymen to develop the artistic potential of the 35mm format.

Woman winnowing rice, 1952

Workers in a Peking carpet factory, 1965

Bueno's 1930 photograph of the arrival of the Graf Zeppelin in Rio de Janeiro

One of his best photographs was the picture above, in which he caught the great dirigible *Graf Zeppelin* on its first trip to Rio, in 1930, filling the sky with what one Rio correspondent described as "the slow majesty of a king."

Nancy Newhall 1908-1974

Nancy Newhall spent more than 30 years setting words to pictures and editing the work of great American photographers for exhibition and publication. Many of the 22 volumes she wrote or edited were exaltations of the American wilderness. Ironically, her life was ended by an accident in the outdoors she loved so much: a spruce tree toppled from an eroded slope onto the raft on which she was floating down the Snake River in Wyoming's Grand Teton National Park.

Newhall helped establish photography as a pre-eminent art form. During World War II, while her husband, Beaumont Newhall, was on military service, she filled in for him as curator of photography at the Museum of Modern Art in New York City. In that capacity, in 1945, she organized the first major retrospective show ever given a photographer by the museum; the photographer was the wide-ranging pioneer Paul Strand. Her best-known book was *This Is the American Earth* (1960), which she edited with Ansel Adams; it included her own free-verse text and was a publishing landmark in the cause of conservation.

Luiz Bueno Filho 1904-1974

Little known outside Brazil but honored in his native country as the dean of its photojournalists, Luiz Bueno Filho died on August 6 at the age of 70 in Rio de Janeiro. Up to six weeks before his death, he was shooting pictures for a newspaper, as he had done for more than 50 years. In the course of that long career Bueno almost single-handedly brought modern photo reporting to Brazil. His vigorous, candid photographs persuaded editors to drop posed shots of ceremonial functions in favor of informative pictures.

The photojournalist-to-be went to work at the age of eight, in 1912, on the day after his mother's funeral; his father, having no one to look after the boy, took him to his office at the Rio newspaper *Correio da Manhã*. At 16 Bueno officially joined the staff as a full-time photographer. In his early years Bueno worked the police beat, lugging a huge Goerz/Anschütz press camera and shooting by the light of magnesium-flash powder. "As soon as you took the picture the room was filled with the smoke of the devil," he once recalled. "But the camera did work."

A true *carioca* (resident of Rio), Bueno hardly ever left the city he loved. He did not need to. In Rio alone he recorded almost all the newsworthy events of Brazil during the half century since World War I.

 Miscellany

Photojournalism on Fifth Avenue

The renaissance of a threatened profession — photojournalism — is the aim of a new photography museum opened on New York's Fifth Avenue in November 1974. The International Center of Photography was founded primarily to support photography that reflects concern for man and his environment, says its director, Cornell Capa, who fears that the photojournalist has become an endangered species with the decline of large general-interest magazines like LIFE and *Look*.

The Center offers galleries where fine documentary pictures can be

Cornell Capa lectures at the Center.

seen, classrooms and laboratories for teaching, and archives to preserve negatives and prints. It has already drawn upon its extensive archives to produce picture books by masters of documentary photography. Two published in 1974 dealt with Roman Vishniac's pictures of Jews in eastern European ghettos on the eve of World War II and Lewis W. Hine's photographs of the brutal toll taken on Americans of the early 20th Century by poverty and industrialization.

The Center made its debut amid a flurry of publicity. In 10 days 10,000 people trooped through the landmark six-story townhouse. They were attracted mainly by two exhibitions: "Classics of Documentary Photography," and a show of pictures by Henri Cartier-Bresson. The Cartier-Bresson display included photographs taken during his first trip to the U.S.S.R. nearly 20 years ago as well as a selection from his recent visit (see the report on his new book, *About Russia,* pages 216-221). The publicity-wise Capa also lured crowds by snaring prominent visitors. Jacqueline Onassis was there, generously posing for dozens of amateur and professional picture-takers and also granting a television interview. Henri Cartier-Bresson also attended, but he proved a reluctant celebrity. Because he believes being photographed would make him too well known to continue taking candid pictures, he has always fled the still

camera. During an interview about his one-man show, he proved equally wary of the TV cameras, and preserved his anonymity by keeping his back turned to the viewers.

A Photo Fair for Russia

Now Soviet Russia can be added to the list of countries acknowledging the importance of photography with a major exposition: The First National Scientific and Practical Conference on the Art of Photography and Photojournalism is scheduled to be held in Moscow in November 1975. The U.S.S.R. thus joins the United States, France, and Japan, which arrange at least one yearly meeting each, and West Germany and Czechoslovakia, which hold theirs every other year.

Moscow's fair will be organized by the Union of Soviet Journalists, which is composed of nearly 60,000 professionals from the various fields of journalism, including virtually all of the U.S.S.R.'s estimated 11,000 professional photographers. Most of the photographers are staff members of publications like the weekly picture magazine *Ogonyok,* or the Communist party daily newspaper, *Pravda.* The 79-member photography commission of the Union, in keeping with its original aim of rendering "creative assistance" to photographers, has been underwriting regional photo fairs in the U.S.S.R. since it was formed in 1959, but never before has it undertaken an official, nationwide gathering.

Unlike most other fairs, the Soviet conference will ignore equipment. Instead, hundreds of press photographers, art experts, technicians, and historians are scheduled to get together to discuss topics ranging from the problems of news photography to theories of esthetic principles. The major exhibition of the fair will be devoted to the work of Siberian photographers, both professional and amateur.

The 1975 conference is limited to Russians. "It is our first venture," said a spokesman for the photography commission, "but when it becomes traditional we shall gladly invite foreign colleagues."

Hank Aaron's Home Run

On April 8, 1974, when Hank Aaron took a crack at his 715th home run, the one that would break Babe Ruth's lifetime record, more than 100 photographers were on hand at Atlanta Stadium, very likely setting a record themselves for pictures taken at a baseball game. Trying for a unique interpretation of the event amid all this competition were two veteran photographers who had worked for LIFE: Ralph Morse and Henry Groskinsky.

They planned a multiple exposure that would show in a single frame Aaron performing five key steps of the achievement: hitting the ball, touching each of the three bases and returning in triumph to the dugout. Morse and Groskinsky set up a 4 x 5 view camera on a heavy tripod in the press section between home plate and first base. They put a plate of glass 14 inches in front of the lens and draped a black cloth from the glass to the camera to prevent reflections. The glass itself was covered with cardboard that had five holes in it, each covered with a flap. One hole vignetted a view of home plate only, the others views of each base and a spot in front of the dugout. The photographers determined the distance between camera and cardboard, and then the placement of the vignette holes in a day-long process of trial and error.

During the game, each time Aaron faced a pitch, Morse made a first exposure. When Aaron finally hit the home run in the fourth inning, Groskinsky had five and a half seconds —the time it took Aaron to reach first base—to close the flap over the first hole and open the second one so that Morse could release the shutter again. The photographers had a little more time—six seconds —to prepare themselves for Aaron's arrival at second base. "After that," says Morse, "we were all right because he slowed down to a jog. In fact, we had to wait 20 minutes between the shot on third and the one near the dugout because it took him that long to get through the crowd at home plate."

Morse and Groskinsky's multiple exposure of Hank Aaron's 715th, 1974

Kennerly's official portrait of President Ford, 1974

The President and Kennerly together

Two Presidents' Photographers

Wearing dungarees and a plaid shirt, a bearded 27-year-old photographer wanders freely about the White House in Washington, casually opening the door of the Oval Office at any hour to chronicle the daily activities of the President of the United States. On the steps of the Elysée Palace in Paris, a spritely octogenarian who describes himself as a scatterbrain shoots a few pictures to make the official portrait of the President of France. Two more radically different choices for official photographers of national leaders could hardly be imagined.

Unflamboyant Gerald Ford chose as his official personal photographer David Hume Kennerly, a brash daredevil who won a Pulitzer Prize at 25 for battlefront pictures of the Vietnam War. Valéry Giscard d'Estaing, who wants to run France like a corporation, invited impish Jacques-Henri Lartigue, 80, to take the official portrait. Both choices were unexpected—particularly that of Lartigue, who started his career at the age of seven with photographs that resemble stills from an absurd but beautiful home movie.

As Lartigue tells the story, the newly elected Giscard simply telephoned him one day and asked, "Would you like to take my photograph?" Lartigue replied, "Mr. Pres-

Lartigue snaps French presidential portrait.

Lartigue's undoctored portrait of President Giscard d'Estaing, 1974

ident, I am sorry, but certainly not. It is not my kind of work, I take pictures for fun." But the persuasive Giscard prevailed.

At the picture-making session, Lartigue asked the President to stand in front of a hanging tricolor, quickly shot a roll and a half, and declared the job done. The result was what Giscard had wanted—"a happy picture," in a business suit rather than the traditional white tie and tails. But in a move typical of French bureaucracy, the version that will hang in the office of every French mayor was retouched. The red band of the French tricolor has been moved to the left from its position in the original, shown on the opposite page.

The relationship between President Ford and David Kennerly is more like that of father and son. For 10 months, while Ford served as Vice President, Kennerly covered his activities for TIME. The day after President Ford was sworn in, Kennerly was adopted into the official family—with the understanding that he would have total access to the President. As unobtrusive as "a flower on the White House wallpaper," he went to work in his new $32,000-a-year job. In the course of his 16-hour workday, Kennerly shoots about 10 rolls of film.

The official portrait on the opposite page, made in the Oval Office during the third week of Ford's Presidency, was the photographer's first formal portrait.

World Cup soccer pictures on Photokina wall

Detail of wall, showing Indian women playing soccer

Photokina's Soccer Wall

Of all the exhibitions at the 1974 Photokina, Cologne's international photography fair, which presented the art of some of the world's outstanding photographers, the single most popular show turned out to be an assortment of soccer-related photographs taken by anonymous snapshooters. Five thousand pictures were mounted cheek by jowl to form a rich, mosaic-like mural with a circle of finalists at the center *(left, top)*. Every one of these photographs had something to do with the quadrennial international soccer tournament held in West Germany in 1974, a series of 38 games to decide the winner of the fiercely contested World Cup.

That so many pictures came to be taken because of some soccer games was the inspiration of a television station in West Germany, where both soccer fever and photography fever run high. The station sponsored a contest called Around the World Cup, which aroused the interest of Photokina.

What the sponsors thought they would get were incidental events accompanying the games. When they received such pictures as a cow pushing a soccer ball, a baby being bathed on the day of a game, a color sequence of sari-clad Indian women playing soccer *(left, bottom),* Photokina covered an exhibition wall with them.

Boom in Museum Photography

Until 1974, permanent museum collections of photography as fine art were nurtured mainly by a few big-city institutions. Now this monopoly has ended. Major collections of prints and negatives have been established all around the United States—among other places, in Atlanta, Baltimore, Pittsburgh, and Sun Valley, Idaho.

The new collections turn out to be different from those of older museums in a number of ways that reflect their locations. In the northwest, for example, the photography department of the Sun Valley Center for the Arts, which opened in May 1974, specializes in photography of the American West. Already purchased are 20 volumes of Edward Curtis's turn-of-the-century photographs of Indian life, and numerous tintypes and daguerreotypes from the days of the Wild West.

The impetus for this expansion came partly from public interest in photography as art, partly from a new generation of aggressive curators. Photography came to Atlanta's High Museum of Art when the director, Gudmund Vigtel, invited A. D. Coleman, a photography critic of the New York *Times,* to lecture before a Thursday night audience. When Coleman finished, said Vigtel, the audience of 500 ended up "yelling their heads off for more."

Vigtel decided to purchase photographs for the first time in the history of the museum. Among more conventional choices, he acquired 10 prints by Paul Kwilecki, from Bainbridge, Georgia, who has concentrated on the life of rural blacks, along with 18 by the celebrated black photographer of Harlem life, James Van Der Zee *(below).*

Such prize collections have been assembled by shrewd dealing by young curators. At the University of

EDWARD L. BAFFORD: *Johnny Appleseed,* 1938

Maryland Baltimore County, Director Antonio Raimo bought some 10,000 prints and 500 glass negatives by the early 20th Century photographer, Lewis W. Hine. Raimo paid $100,000 for the Hine cache; since half the prints were duplicates, he traded them for other pictures worth the entire $100,000. The university wound up with the material at no cost.

Raimo has proved equally adept at rescuing neglected talent. One 1974 acquisition and subsequent show in Baltimore brought belated recognition to Edward L. Bafford, whose idyllic views of Maryland *(above),* printed in the antique bromoil process, show the affection and insight of a lifelong resident.

JAMES VAN DER ZEE: *Jazz Age Harlem couple,* 1932

Bibliography

General

Editors of TIME-LIFE BOOKS, *Life Library of Photography*, TIME-LIFE BOOKS, 1970-1972.

Focal Press, *The Focal Encyclopedia of Photography*. Focal Press, 1965.

Friedman, Joseph S., *History of Color Photography*. The American Photographic Publishing Company, 1944.

Gernsheim, Helmut, *Creative Photography*. Faber & Faber, 1962.

Gernsheim, Helmut and Alison, *The History of Photography from the Camera Obscura to the Beginning of the Modern Era*. McGraw-Hill, 1969.

Newhall, Beaumont, *The History of Photography*. The Museum of Modern Art, 1964.

Special Essays

Adams, Ansel, and Nancy Newhall, *This Is the American Earth*. Sierra Club and Ballantine Books, 1968.

Annual of Advertising and Editorial Art (1930-1940). The Art Directors Club.

Art Deco. Finch College Museum of Art, 1970.

Baumeister, Philip, and Gerald Pincus, "Optical Interference Coatings," *Scientific American*, December 1970.

Beaton, Cecil, *Photobiography*. Doubleday & Company, 1951.

Bruce, David, *Sun Pictures*. New York Graphic Society, 1973.

Cameron, Julia Margaret, *Victorian Photographs of Famous Men & Fair Women*. David R. Godine, 1973.

Cartier-Bresson, Henri:
The Decisive Moment. Simon & Schuster, 1952.
The Europeans. Simon & Schuster, 1955.
People of Moscow. Simon & Schuster, 1955.

Chase, Edna Woolman and Ilka, *Always In Vogue*. Doubleday & Company, 1954.

Cunningham, Imogen, *Imogen!* University of Washington Press, 1974.
Photographs by Imogen Cunningham. University of Washington Press, 1970.

Doisneau, Robert:
Les Parisiens Tels Qu'ils Sont. Collection "Huit," 1954.
Le Point Bistrots. Souillac-Mulhouse, 1960.

Frank, Waldo, et al., *America & Alfred Stieglitz: A Collective Portrait*. Doubleday, Doran & Company, 1934.

Heavens, O. S., *Optical Properties of Thin Solid Films*. Dover Publications, 1965.

Hillier, Bevis, *Art Deco*. Studio Vista Limited and E. P. Dutton, 1968.

Horst, *Salute To The Thirties*. Viking Press, 1971.

Hoyningen-Huene. University of Southern California, Los Angeles, 1970.

James, T. H., ed., *The Theory of the Photographic Process*. The Macmillan Company, 1966.

Kosar, Jaromir, *Light-Sensitive Systems*. John Wiley & Sons, 1965.

Laughlin, Clarence John:
Clarence John Laughlin: The Personal Eye. Aperture, 1973.
Ghosts Along The Mississippi. Crown Publishing, 1962.

Lartigue, Jacques-Henri:
Diary of a Century. Viking Press, 1970.
---and Jean Fondin, *Boyhood Photos of J.-H. Lartigue*. Ami Guichard, 1966.

Levin, Phyllis Lee, *The Wheels of Fashion*. Doubleday & Company, 1965.

Lewis, Steven, et al., *Photography, Source and Resource*. Turnip Press, 1973.

Lothrop, Eaton S., Jr., *A Century of Cameras*. Morgan & Morgan, 1973.

Moore, Peter, "The New World of Resin-Coated Papers," *Photo Methods for Industry*, March 1974.

"Multicoating Hysteria," *Optical News Industry*, July-August 1973.

Newhall, Nancy:
P. H. Emerson. Aperture, 1975.
Time in New England: Photographs by Paul Strand. Oxford University Press, 1950.

Nickolas Muray. International Museum of Photography at George Eastman House, 1974.

Sembach, Klaus-Jurgen, *Style 1930*. Universe Books, 1971.

Snow, Carmel, with Mary Louise Aswell, *The World of Carmel Snow*. McGraw-Hill, 1962.

Steichen, Edward, *A Life in Photography*. Doubleday & Company, 1963.

White, Minor, *mirrors messages manifestations*. Aperture, 1969.

Periodicals

Afterimage. Visual Studies Workshop, Rochester, New York.

Aperture. Aperture, Millerton, New York.

Artweek. Oakland, California.

Asahi Camera. Asahi Shimbun, Tokyo, Japan.

The British Journal of Photography. Henry Greenwood, London, England.

Camera. C. J. Bucher, Lucerne, Switzerland.

Camera Mainichi '74. The Mainichi Newspapers, Tokyo, Japan.

Camera 35. American Express Publishing, New York City.

Creative Camera. Coo Press, London, England.

Fotographia Italiana. Editphoto, Milan, Italy.

Harper's Bazaar. The Hearst Corporation, New York City.

impressions. impressions, Toronto, Canada.

Interview. Motion Olympus, New York City.

Modern Photography. Billboard Publications, New York City.

National Geographic Magazine. National Geographic Society, Washington, D.C.

Nueva Lente. Madrid, Spain.

Photographic Trade News. PTN Publishing, Hempstead, New York.

Photo World (1973-1974). Photo Journal, New York City.

Popular Photography. Ziff-Davis Publishing, New York City.

Rolling Stone. Straight Arrow Publishers, San Francisco.

Smithsonian. Smithsonian Associates, Washington, D.C.

Vogue. Condé Nast Publications, New York City.

Zoom. Publicness, Paris, France.

Acknowledgments

For their help, the editors are indebted to Peter C. Bunnell, Princeton University, N.J. and Harvey S. Zucker, New York City. The editors also wish to thank:

In the Americas—Richard C. Babish, Perkin-Elmer Corp., Norwalk, Conn.; Philip Baumeister, Institute of Optics, Univ. of Rochester, N.Y.; Paul Binai, Carnegie Institute, Pittsburgh, Pa.; Eldio Bueno, Rio de Janeiro, Brazil; David Butwin, New York City; Cornell Capa, International Center of Photography, New York City; Peter Chaitin, Englewood, N.J.; Robert Chapman, Unicolor, Inc., Dexter, Michigan; Toby Chiu, New York City; James L. Chung, Fuji Photo Film U.S.A., Inc., New York City; Louise Dahl-Wolfe, Frenchtown, N.J.; Peter Daidone, Berkey Marketing Companies, Inc., New York City; Scott Graphics, Inc., Holyoke, Massachusetts; Michael Drons, Spruce Head, Maine; Cliff Edom, School of Journalism, Univ. of Missouri, Columbia; Stanley Eisenman, Eisenman & Enock, Inc., New York City; Walter Ferber, Hanimex (U.S.A.) Inc., New York City; Christine Fiorelli, Massachusetts Institute of Technology, Cambridge; Ronald Francis, Rochester Institute of Technology, N.Y.;

Irwin Friedman, Perkin-Elmer Corp., Norwalk, Conn.; Thomas H. Garver, M. H. de Young Memorial Museum, San Francisco; Bill Giordano, Ehrenreich Photo-Optical Industries, Inc., Garden City, N.Y.; Suzanne Goldstein, Rapho Guillumette, New York City; Fred Handsman, Berkey Marketing Co., Inc., New York City; Harold C. Harsh, Kalvar Corp., New Orleans; Cheri Hiser, Sun Valley Center for the Arts, Idaho; Michael E. Hoffman, Aperture Inc., Millerton, N.Y.; Jon Holmes, Polaroid Corp., Cambridge, Mass.; Horst, Oyster Bay, N.Y.; Matthew Isenberg, Hadlyme, Conn.; John P. Januzik, Ponder & Best, Inc., Santa Monica, Cal.; Lora Jones, E. R. Squibb & Sons, Inc., Princeton, N.J.; Herbert Keppler and Horoshi Kimata, *Modern Photography*, New York City; J. Roy King, Eastman Kodak Company, Rochester, N.Y.; Lillian King, Hesperia, Cal.; Fred Knubel, Columbia University, New York City; James Kunz, Luminos Photo Corp., Yonkers, N.Y.; Wilbur George Kurtz, Jr., The Coca-Cola Company, Atlanta, Ga.; Janet Lehr, New York City; Walter J. Lekki, Optical Coating Laboratory, Inc., Santa Rosa, Cal.; Steven Lobel, State Photo Supply Corp., Albany,

N.Y.; Richard Lo Pinto, Ehrenreich Photo-Optical Industries, Inc., Garden City, N.Y.; Eaton S. Lothrop, Jr., The Collegiate School, New York City; Kurt Luhn, Minox Corp., New York City; Harry Lunn, Lunn Gallery, Washington, D.C.; Donlyn Lyndon, Massachusetts Institute of Technology, Cambridge; Noel Manfre, Joseph E. Seagram & Sons, Inc., New York City; Harold Martin, New York City; Pat McCabe, Irving Penn Studios, New York City; Denise McCluggage, Warren, Vt.; William McKenna, Braun North America, Cambridge, Mass.; Scott Mlyn, New York City; Beaumont Newhall, University of New Mexico, Albuquerque; Robert Norwick, E. T. Howard Co., Inc., New York City; David L. Ohlson, Rollei of America, Inc., Fairfield, N.J.; Eugene Ostroff and Harry Patton, Smithsonian Institution, Washington, D.C.; Antonio R. Raimo, University of Maryland Baltimore County, Baltimore; Evelyn Raphael, The Condé Nast Publications, New York City; Andrea Rawle, Carmel, Cal.; George Rinhart, New York City; Arnold Saks, New York City; Leslie Segal, Corporate Annual Reports, Inc., New York City; Ken Shirahata, Asahi Optical America, Inc., New York

City; Byron and Mary Shumaker, The Washington Gallery of Photography, Washington, D.C.; Robert A. Sobieszek, International Museum of Photography at George Eastman House, Rochester, N.Y.; Michael D. Sullivan, Eastman Kodak Company, Rochester, N.Y.; Kathy Tindle, The White House, Washington, D.C.; John B. Turnbull, Horizons Research Inc., Cleveland, Ohio; Gudmund Vigtel, High Museum of Art, Atlanta, Ga.; Ora Vesta Watson, Natchitoches, Louisiana; Allen and Hilary Weiner, New York City; F. H. Wemple, Handy & Harmon, New York City; Caroline Wistar, Philadelphia Museum of Art, Pa.;

Lee Witkin, The Witkin Gallery, New York City; Grant Wolfkill, E. R. Squibb & Sons, Inc., Princeton, N.J.; Helen Wright, New York City.

In Asia—Takeyoshi Tanuma, Tokyo.

In Europe—Philippe Alemand, Paris; Michel Auer, Geneva; Georges Bardawill, *Le Nouveau Photocinéma,* Paris; Sue Davies, The Photographers Gallery, London; Michel Decron, *Photo,* Paris; Les Editeurs Français Réunis, Paris; Oreste Ferrari and Anna Ghelli, Gabinetto Fotografico Nazionale, Rome; Philippe Garner, Sotheby's Belgravia, London; Pierre Gassman, Pictorial Service, Paris; C. H. Gibbs-Smith, The

National Portrait Gallery, London; L. Fritz Gruber, Photokina, Cologne; Léon Herschtritt, Paris; Guy Knoché, Editorial Service, Documentation Français, Paris; Barry Lane, The Arts Council of Great Britain, London; Jean-Claude Lemagny, Bibliothèque Nationale, Paris; Hans-Wilhelm Leckscheidt, Rollei-Werke Franke & Heidecke, Braunschweig, West Germany; Pier-Paolo Preti, Modena, Italy; Dr. Joachim Pump, Agfa-Gevaert AG, Leverkusen, West Germany; Arturo Quintavalle, Instituto di Storia dell'Arte, University of Parma, Italy; Gail Ridgwell, London; Fabienne de Sèze, Musée des Arts Décoratifs, Paris.

Picture Credits *Credits from left to right are separated by semicolons, from top to bottom by dashes.*

COVER—Paulus Leeser, lens courtesy Ponder & Best, Inc.; Hans Feurer.

The Major Shows: 11—Branko Lenart Jr. 13 —Francisco Hidalgo. 14—Bruno Barbey. 15, 16, 17—Hans Feurer. 18—Michael Abramson. 19 —Tassilo Trost. 20, 21—Tomas Sennett. 24, 25 —Kenneth Graves. 26, 27—Crawford Barton. 28 —Ellen Brooks. 29—Gary Stewart. 30, 31—Leslie Poliak. 32, 33—William Messer. 35—Arthur Grace, *The New York Times.* 36, 37—Carl Leavitt, from *Celebrations,* published by Aperture, Inc., Millerton, New York; Imogen Cunningham. 38, 39—Michael Kaufman, from *Celebrations,* published by Aperture, Inc., Millerton, New York. 40, 41—Terry Reed. 42—John Loori. 43—Siegfried Halus. 44, 45 —Minor White. 46 through 54—Copyright © 1973 by Clarence John Laughlin, from *Clarence John Laughlin: The Personal Eye,* published by Aperture, Inc., Millerton, New York.

The Marketplace: 57—Jay Maisel, courtesy PepsiCo, Inc. 60—Evelyn Hofer. Original photographs by Charles P. Reay; Evelyn Hofer —Alexandre Georges, courtesy E. R. Squibb & Sons, Inc. Original photographs: center left, Ernst Haas; right center, Brian Brake from Rapho Guillumette. 63—Richard Avedon, courtesy Ultima II—Charles Revson. 64—Burt Glinn from Magnum, courtesy PepsiCo, Inc. 65 —Harald Sund, courtesy Louisiana-Pacific Corporation. 66, 67—Co Rentmeester, courtesy Pfizer Inc.; Ron Barnett, courtesy Wallace Murray Corporation. 68—Jay Maisel. 69—Gary Gladstone, courtesy HCA-Martin, Inc. 70, 71 —George E. Watson; Bruce Davidson from Magnum, courtesy Corning Glass Works. 76 —Derek Bayes, courtesy Anthony Wigram. 77 —Leif Preus—Print by Derek Bayes from curved glass negative of Sutton camera in collection of Anthony Wigram. 78, 79—Paulus Leeser, courtesy Matthew Isenberg. Pages 80 through 84 except page 83 copied by Paulus Leeser. 80—James Gardner, courtesy Janet Lehr. 81 —Wood and Gibson, courtesy Janet Lehr. 82 —James Gardner, courtesy Janet Lehr. 83 —Julia Margaret Cameron, courtesy Sotheby's Belgravia. 84—Hill and Adamson, courtesy George Rinhart.

The New Technology: 87—Enrico Ferorelli. 89 —Ken Kay. 91—Neil Kagan; Drawing by Nicholas Fasciano. 92—Canon U.S.A., Inc. —Drawings by Nicholas Fasciano, original

courtesy Canon U.S.A., Inc. 93—Minolta Corporation; Ponder & Best, Inc.—Drawing by Nicholas Fasciano, original courtesy Perkin-Elmer Corporation—Al Freni, lens courtesy Ponder & Best, Inc.; Nikon, Inc. 96 through 99 —Drawings by Nicholas Fasciano. 105 —Negative copied by Ken Kay. Drawing by Nicholas Fasciano. 106—Drawing by Nicholas Fasciano. 107—Al Freni; Drawings by Nicholas Fasciano. 108—Rollei; Ernst Leitz GmbH; Canon, Inc. 109—Fuji Photo Film Co., Ltd.; Ponder & Best, Inc.; Minox GmbH. 110—Bettina Gruber; Kowa Company, Ltd. 111—Al Freni; Steve Fenn. 112—Joe Harris, courtesy Ilford Limited; E.P.O.I., Inc. and Durst. 113—Braun North America; Joe Harris, courtesy Ilford Limited. 114—Jos. Schneider & Co.; Karl Heitz, Inc. and Gitzo; Paterson Products Ltd.

Discoveries: 117—Williams Scurani; Glenda Milrod—Anders Birkeland from Saftra; Tom Eckstrom; Carlo Stella. 119—Giorgio Lotti; Walter Daran from Time-Life Picture Agency —Dorothy Thompson; Courtesy Sven Andersson —Sonia Sheridan; John Reeves. 120—Carlo Stella. 121 through 125—Franco Fontana. 126 —Glenda Milrod. 127 through 131—Shin Sugino. 132—Anders Birkeland from Saftra. 133 through 137—Anders Petersen from Saftra. 138 —Williams Scurani. 139 through 145—Luigi Ghirri. 146—Tom Eckstrom. 147 through 154 —Dennis Hearne.

Trends: 157—Edward Steichen, copyright © 1931 (renewed 1959) by The Condé Nast Publications Inc., copied by Paulus Leeser. 159, 165—George Hoyningen-Huene, copyright © 1931 (renewed 1959) by The Condé Nast Publications Inc., copied by Paulus Leeser, courtesy Sonnabend Gallery and Horst. 163 —Margaret Bourke-White, courtesy Margaret Bourke-White estate. 166, 168—George Hoyningen-Huene, copyright © 1932 (renewed 1960) by The Condé Nast Publications Inc., copied by Paulus Leeser, courtesy Sonnabend Gallery and Horst. 167—George Hoyningen-Huene, copyright © 1933 (renewed 1961) by The Condé Nast Publications Inc., copied by Paulus Leeser, courtesy Sonnabend Gallery and Horst. 169—George Hoyningen-Huene, courtesy *Harper's Bazaar,* © The Hearst Corporation, 1936, copied by Paulus Leeser. 170—George Hoyningen-Huene, courtesy *Harper's Bazaar,* © The Hearst Corporation, 1937, courtesy Horst. 171—Horst, copyright © 1934 (renewed 1962) by The Condé Nast Publications Inc., copied by Paulus Leeser, courtesy Sonnabend Gallery. 172

—Horst, copyright © 1938 (renewed 1966) by The Condé Nast Publications Inc., copied by Paulus Leeser, courtesy Sonnabend Gallery. 173 —Horst, copyright © 1936 (renewed 1964) by The Condé Nast Publications Inc. 174, 175 —Cecil Beaton, copyright © 1935 (renewed 1963) by The Condé Nast Publications Inc., copied by Paulus Leeser. 177, 178, 179 —Nickolas Muray, copied by Paulus Leeser, courtesy International Museum of Photography at George Eastman House. 180—Nickolas Muray, photographed for The Coca-Cola Company, copied by Paulus Leeser, courtesy International Museum of Photography at George Eastman House.

The Annual Awards: 183—Wally McNamee, *Newsweek.* 185—Bruce Dale © National Geographic Society. 186—Giorgio Lotti, *Epoca,* copyright Mondadoripress. 187—Keiichiro Goto, from *Photography I and 2,* published by Aoyagi Shoji K. K. 188—Yoshihiko Shiga, from *Daisetsu,* published by Nichirinsha. 189—Kiyoshi Takai, from *Kura,* published by Kodansha International Ltd. 190—Terutaka Hashimoto, from *Goze,* published by Norasha. 191—Yukichi Watabe, from *Eternal Egypt,* published by Heibonsha. 192—Gina Lollobrigida, from *Italia Mia,* published by Amphoto, Garden City, New York. 193—Pierre Michaud. 194—Raymond Depardon from Gamma—David Burnett from Gamma. 195 —Chas Gerretsen from Gamma. 196—*The New York Times.* 197—Ron Smith, *Bloomington Courier-Tribune* (Indiana). 198—Sal Veder from Wide World. 199—Anthony K. Roberts from Wide World. 200—Peter Jay, *The Sun,* London.

The Year's Books: 203 through 211—Robert Doisneau from Rapho Guillumette. 212 through 215—Irving Penn, copyright © 1974, courtesy The Condé Nast Publications Inc. 216 through 221—Henri Cartier-Bresson. 222, 223—Ansel Adams. 224, 225—Ansel Adams; Ansel Adams, from Portfolio VI, reproduced courtesy Parasol Press, New York.

Roundup: 229, 230—© Ihei Kimura. 231—Luiz Bueno Filho. 232—Marcia Keegan. 233—© Ralph Morse and Henry Groskinsky. 234—David Hume Kennerly, The White House; Chick Harrity from Wide World—Gamma; Jacques-Henri Lartigue D. F. 235—Bettina Gruber—Bettina Gruber. Original color sequence by George Dusius. 236—James Van Der Zee, courtesy High Museum of Art; Edward L. Bafford, courtesy University of Maryland Baltimore County.

Index
A numeral in italics indicates a photograph or drawing of the subject mentioned.

Printed in U.S.A.